Cambridge

OFFICIAL GUIDE

CAMBRIDGE
CITY COUNCIL

ENVIRONMENT
& PLANNING

JARROLD

Outside cover: *Mathematical Bridge, Queens' College*

Acknowledgements

Cambridge City Leisure Services. Maps and walk routes based on original artwork © ESR Limited.

Picture credits

Bell Language Schools: pp. 184, 185; Burghley House, Northamptonshire: p. 169; Cambridge City Council: pp. 14, 22, 113, 138, 140, 141, 154, 167, 186–7; Cambridge Contemporary Art: p. 119; Cambridge Fine Art ('Woodland Pond' by J. Thors): p. 180; Cambridgeshire Collection: pp. 15, 17, 18–19, 28; Cambridge United FC: p. 148 (photo © Cyrus Daboo); Cromwell Museum, Huntingdon: p. 176; John Curtis: pp. 2–3; Findlay Kember: p. 151; Fitzwilliam Museum: pp. 20–1; Garden House Hotel: p. 162; Grafton Centre: p. 134; Heart of the East Millennium Youth Games: p. 150 (Express Pictures © Bob Jones); Imperial War Museum, Duxford: p. 179; Kettle's Yard (by Don Manning): p. 117; National Stud: pp. 172–3; The National Trust Historical Collection: p. 170; Norris Museum, St Ives: p. 177; 'PA' News: pp. 30–1; RSPB: p. 173; Royston Cave: p. 172; Schlumberger Cambridge Research: pp. 26–7; Stained Glass Museum, Ely: p. 178; Twenty-pence Pottery, Wilburton: p. 180; University Arms Hotel: p. 120; Wood Green Animal Shelter: p. 174.

Text by Janet and Michael Jeacock.
Additional information from the Cambridge Tourist Information Centre.

Every effort has been made to ensure that the information given in this book is correct at the time of going to press. However, Jarrold Publishing cannot accept responsibility for any errors or inaccuracies that may appear. The publishers would be grateful to hear from readers about any recent changes which may have taken place.

ISBN 0-7117-0687-5
© Jarrold Publishing 1994, revised and reprinted 1997 and 2000.
Printed in Great Britain. 3/00

Designed and produced by
**Jarrold Publishing
Whitefriars, Norwich NR3 1TR**

CAMBRIDGE OFFICIAL GUIDE

Cambridge

OFFICIAL GUIDE

Contents

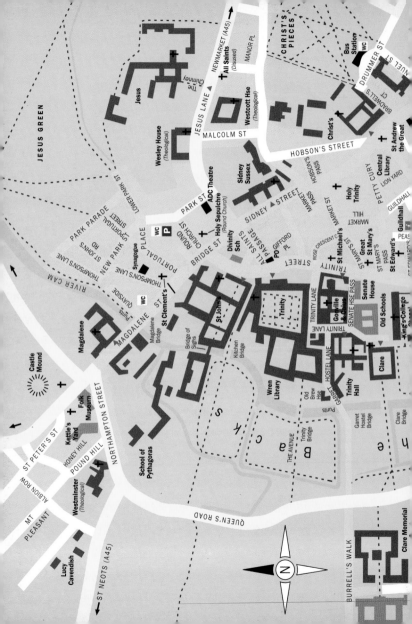

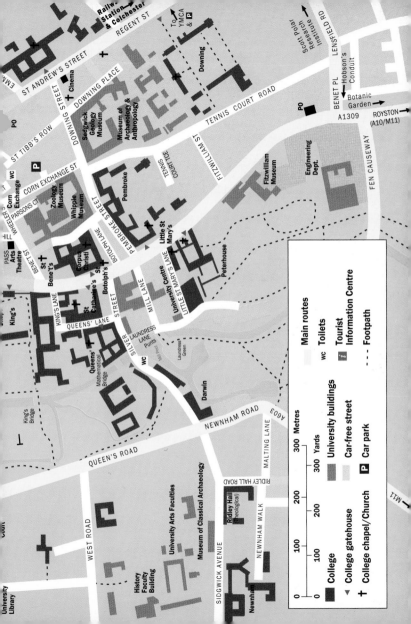

St John's College

Welcome to Cambridge

Punting on the River Cam

The name 'Cambridge' brings instant images to the mind's eye: the breathtaking view of the west end of King's College Chapel from across the river, its Christmas Eve service of Nine Lessons and Carols, thousands of students cycling frantically to their lectures, the Cam packed with punts and the Backs magically carpeted with millions of spring flowers. But Cambridge is more than the sum of its images. It manages to combine happily its roles as historic city with a world-famous university, as a regional centre and, more recently, as the internationally renowned hub of technological, scientific and commercial excellence.

It is impossible, of course, to separate ancient city from ancient university for the two are now inextricably intertwined and they are more at ease with each other than at any time in the past 800 years. For centuries the privileges of the university and the colleges created resentment and ill-will among the townsfolk which, occasionally, spilled over into actual violence. Today 'town and gown' live, work and play together as one harmonious community.

Cambridge — King George VI granted it city status in 1951 — has been careful to control excessive development, and even with expected small boundary changes and increased housing its population is unlikely to be much in excess of 120,000 in the foreseeable future.

Cambridge market from Great St Mary's Church

Nevertheless, the past decade has seen dramatic developments in science-based industry and other areas of employment. Traditionally Cambridge was a market town which just happened to be blessed with the presence, since 1209, of one of the world's greatest universities. With the decline of agriculture, its importance as a market town has diminished – although the largest agricultural machinery sale in the country is held regularly in the city.

Major local employers include Philips Electronic and Associated Industries, the family-owned Marshall Group with its own important airfield, Cambridge University Press, which is the oldest printing-house in the country, building firms of national repute and, of course, Cambridge University and the colleges.

However, it is in the fields of research-related industries and leisure where the major explosion in employment has occurred in recent years. The large Science Park on the Milton side of Cambridge, owned and created by Trinity College, has

Trinity College

The University Chancellor, HRH Prince Philip, in procession

modern, are now heavily involved in the international conference market, using their facilities during vacation time to supplement those which previously existed only in the city's fine hotels. Language schools mainly teaching English as a Foreign Language have also proliferated recently so that thousands of young students from abroad are attracted to the city, their presence adding to the traditional air of youthful gaiety.

Shoppers are superbly catered for with a rich mixture of outlets from the multi-nationals to exquisite craft shops; the city's bookshops are naturally of the very highest quality.

The arts and sport will be dealt with later in this guide but it is surely

attracted such internationally known companies as the Napp Pharmaceutical Group.

The recent realisation by Cambridge University that much of its research has immense commercial value has attracted technology firms of the highest repute to the city – so much so that the city has been dubbed 'Silicon Fen'.

Many of the colleges, both ancient and

true that few, if any, communities of Cambridge's size can boast such a splendid variety of leisure facilities.

Cambridge has welcomed uncountable millions of visitors down the years – and still they will come to enjoy its marvellous mixture of the best of the old and the new, its incredible intellectual and architectural heritage and its ability to say again and again: 'WELCOME TO CAMBRIDGE'. □

Modern Cambridge is epitomised by the architecture of the Napp Laboratories designed by Arthur Erickson (see also p. 27)

The history of Cambridge

King's Parade
*by Louise
Rayner, c. 1887*

A tranquil, slow-running river and a small, insignificant hill were the basic ingredients which created Cambridge. Today the river is called the Cam and the hill is Castle Hill. Together they were responsible for establishing a community which has had nearly two thousand years of continuous existence and whose name is the international synonym for integrity and excellence. This is how it happened ...

Celts, Romans and Saxons

The Roman legions, composed of 'gifted, civilised but ruthless' warriors, had come to conquer Britain forty years after the birth of Christ. They had established their headquarters at Camulodunum — we know it as Colchester — in Essex and immediately busied themselves extending their boundaries of power and building roads along which their armies could move at speed.

On one march northwards they came to our little river. Its gentle current presented no problems and was easily forded. And there, on its left bank and overlooking the river, was a military commander's dream and, in the endless flatlands of East Anglia, almost a miracle — a hill.

Rising to a mere 70 feet *21 m* above sea-level, the hill was nevertheless ideal for defending the river-crossing below and dominated the surrounding area.

Initially, the Romans established a military post on the hill but this was quickly followed by a civil settlement, a rural township of some 25 acres *10 ha* set within a four-sided enclosure and built of clay, wood and thatch. Cambridge became the main centre of the district and remained so for the rest of the three and a half centuries of Roman occupation.

The Romans were not the first visitors but their appearance marked the beginnings of the community proper. There is evidence of earlier peoples who also made use of the river and the hill but it was not until the Late Bronze Age, around 1,000–500 BC, that there was any extensive activity. An excavated gravel pit in Chesterton yielded an important hoard of bronze tools and weapons which would have been used by a pastoral hunting-group.

The area attracted others in the Early Iron Age, about 250–30 BC, when a chariot-using aristocracy, probably from northern France, were here. One of their number comes down to us today — in 1903 in a grave at Newnham Croft on the left bank of the river, the skeleton of a man of rank of that period was found. Buried with him were brooches and a ring which would have been used to pin together the robes of a charioteer.

The south-west view of Cambridge Castle gatehouse, 1818, by J.S. Cotman

Finds, in Chesterton, Cherry Hinton and Madingley Road, of pedestal vases, barrel and butt urns, tell us that 'Belgic' people were here during the first century AD. They, too, had a fortified encampment on the hill.

With the departure of the Romans early in AD 400, the Anglo-Romans left behind found themselves easy prey to invaders because they had become softened by centuries of Roman government and protection by the legions. The Saxons arrived in numbers and although they lived on the hill they also had settlements near Great St Mary's Church and in Trumpington. Grave goods found in cemeteries of the period show that the new invaders had definite connections with Saxon lands between the Weser and the Elbe.

These were pagan times; the dark centuries had arrived. Although Christianity was making its painful introduction to the area, the region was becoming depopulated. So much so that when a group of monks sailed into Cambridge from Ely in the seventh century in search of a stone coffin for the burial of the foundress of their monastery, St Etheldreda, they found the town 'desolate'.

The chaos of the Dark Ages was compounded by the constant warring of the rival kingdoms of Mercia and East Anglia, with Cambridge trapped between the two factions. The dual settlement of Cambridge, with the Mercians on the left bank and the Anglians on the right, was finally united, it is believed, by the building of a bridge by King Offa when he was in overall command of the region.

The Anglo-Saxon Chronicle's annal for AD 875 refers to 'Grantebrycge'. It was the first reference to a bridge at Cambridge and is thought to be the first recorded use of the term 'bridge' in the language.

How did Cambridge get its name?

Despite Cambridge's vast scholarship, the question of how Cambridge got its name is still unanswered and argued over. One thing only is certain. The river was the fount of the community's name. However, for centuries the important name for the river was 'Grant' or 'Granta', not 'Cam' as it is today — the Granta now being regarded as a tributary of the Cam, the main river.

Early chroniclers differed. Bede, about AD 730, had *Grantacaestir*, whilst Felix of Crowland in AD 745 wrote of *Grontricc*. Then, in the Anglo-Saxon Chronicle annal for 875, we find

Grantebrycge – the first coupling of river name and bridge. Coins minted in the town between 979 and 1100 bore the name *Grant*, *Grante* or *Granti*. In 1050 Guthlac knew the town as *Grante-ceaster*, but from 1107 the town was referred to variously as *Cantabrigia* (the Latinised name for Cambridge), *Caumbrigge*, *Caumbrege* or *Camberage* and, in 1478, *Camebrygge*. By Elizabethan times it was *Cambridge*.

The best-known of all the variations appeared in the first line of Chaucer's *Reeve's Tale* in the late fourteenth century: 'At Trumpington, not fer fro Cantebrigge ...'.

Internal wranglings between the English kingdoms were to be overshadowed by a menacing external threat, so the kingdoms began to unite in the face of the new danger.

Invasion by the Vikings

East Anglia was particularly vulnerable to the sea-faring Danes and Norsemen, who were able to probe deep inland in their boats on the region's many rivers.

From 865 a Danish army had ravaged at will in the area, and in 875 the Anglo-Saxon Chronicle recorded that the invading army wintered at Cambridge. The town was easily reached by the Vikings because the river was tidal to within 9 miles *14.5 km* of the town and easily navigable thereafter. In 878 the whole of eastern England from the Thames to Teesside and, of course, including Cambridge, passed into the Danelaw.

Despite the savagery for which the Vikings are best remembered, they were also ingenious traders, and Cambridge was to prosper mightily because of this fact for centuries to come.

The Danes established themselves on the right bank of the river within a few yards of where the Romans had first crossed 800 years earlier. Here they built a port complete with hythes (landing-places) and wharves. Cambridge became solidly entrenched as the chief centre of the county. Here commerce prospered, and the town grew.

The Anglo-Danish town centred on that area of Bridge Street in which St Clement's Church — Clement was the patron saint of Danish sailors — stands. The hill on the left bank had become commercially

St Bene't's Church tower

unimportant, and it was the right-bank traders of the inland seaport who created wealth.

The Danelaw continued until early in the tenth century, when Edward the Elder, King of Wessex, recovered the region for the Saxons. He was not able to prevent further Viking incursions, however, and in 1010 the wood and thatch town of Cambridge was put to the torch just before the final Danish conquest by King Canute (or Cnut). He restored order, the town was rebuilt and from the wealth created by the sailing traders the first stone buildings began to rise above the humble wooden buildings of the town. One of them, the tower of St Bene't's Church still stands solid and proud as it was when the Saxons built it about 1025.

The Vikings then, with their genius for trade, made Cambridge the chief town in the county (it was the Danelaw which divided the country into shires and counties), a position it continues to hold to this day.

Norman conquest

In 1027, across the English Channel, an illegitimate son was born to the Duke of Normandy and a tanner's daughter. He was named William. He succeeded his father and determined to take the throne of England from Harold. William defeated the English army at Hastings, where Harold was slain by a fateful arrow, and the Conqueror was crowned on Christmas Day 1066. His rule, stern but orderly, was to change the face of England, not least in Cambridge ...

It was two years after Hastings that Cambridge found itself affected by the Conqueror. After accepting the surrender of York, William marched south in 1068, raising castles at Lincoln, Huntingdon — and on the hill by the Cam in Cambridge. Twenty-seven houses were demolished in

Cambridge Prison and Castle, the print by Ackermann, 1815

the Castle Hill area to make way for the motte-and-bailey structure. It controlled the waterway, commanded the bridge and dominated the town. It also looked out across the sulphurous wastes of the Fen country to the north, where rebellion, led by Hereward the Wake, was stirring. The Saxons in their swampy stronghold in the Fens were supposedly betrayed by treacherous monks at Ely who led the Conqueror's men to the insurgents. The Normans snuffed out the rebellion with severity.

With the coming of the Norman castle, law and order in Cambridge passed from leading local trading families into royal hands in the person of the king's sheriff, Picot. His hand lay heavy on the people, and one townsman called him 'a hungry lion, a ravening wolf, a filthy hog'.

Nevertheless, he increased the town's commercial and ecclesiastical importance by building three mills and establishing a house of regular canons which included a church dedicated to St Giles. Later this foundation moved from the castle area to Barnwell, became a house of Augustinian canons and was to have profound influence on the community throughout the Middle Ages.

Cambridge Market Place *by F. Mackenzie, 1841, with Hobson's Conduit*

The town continued to prosper – even more so when King Henry I forbade ships to discharge at any other hythe in the shire than Cambridge and that toll should be taken there and there only.

Religion and trade

It was not just commerce that was turning Cambridge into a national jewel. Its ecclesiastical prominence continued to

grow throughout the twelfth century. A house of Benedictine nuns was established, the buildings of which form the nucleus of Jesus College. Two hospitals, run by monks, were founded: the Leper Hospital outside the town and the Hospital of St John in the town centre. The exquisite Leper Chapel of St Mary Magdalene still stands alongside the Newmarket Road beyond Barnwell, and the foundations of St John's Hospital can be seen in the first court of St John's College.

The finest building bequeathed to Cambridge by the Normans is the Round Church of the Holy Sepulchre, near the site of the original Danish settlement. The oldest surviving secular house in Cambridge is the 'School of Pythagoras' (about 1200), which stands in the grounds of St John's College.

The mendicant orders flocked to Cambridge, bringing with them accumulated wisdom and, importantly, teaching. The Franciscans came in 1226, settling finally on the site of Sidney Sussex College, the Dominicans settled in what is now Emmanuel College, the Carmelites were in Chesterton in 1249 until moving into the town near King's College, and then there were the Friars of the Sack, the Austin Friars, the Friars of St Mary and, not least, the Gilbertine Canons of Sempringham.

All was not stern religion, however. Annually, from the early 1200s, Cambridge hosted one of the greatest trading fairs in Europe, Barnwell Fair. To the fair each August and September came merchants bearing silks and wines, leather goods, horses, fish, meat, books and ironware. Traders in tin came from Cornwall and wool merchants from all over East Anglia. Throughout the fair there was much roistering — drinking-booths were set up, there was theatre and bear-baiting. The fair brought national fame to Cambridge, and centuries later Good Queen Bess was to declare it 'by far the largest and most famous fair in all England'. And so it continued until well into the eighteenth century.

So Cambridge slipped easily into the thirteenth century, prosperous, learned and with a national and, indeed, a European reputation. The medieval town had precise boundaries and was contained within the King's Ditch to the east and south, a defensive device dug 200 years earlier with the river forming the north and west boundary. Gradually the castle was assuming its final medieval form with towers, a gatehouse, a hall and various chambers.

In 1201 and 1207 King John granted charters establishing the town as a corporation. These were plainly significant times, but the townsfolk, the merchants, the boatmen, the monks, nuns, beggars and lepers had no inkling that it was to be the most momentous century in the history of Cambridge. For the early thirteenth century was to see the beginnings of the university which was to bring intellectual and architectural glory to Cambridge over the forthcoming 800 years.

Birth of the university

Later, this guide will examine the history and development of the University of Cambridge and the colleges in detail, but certain events were of such immense importance to both 'town and gown' that they are inseparable.

It is to Oxford that we have to turn momentarily to study the beginnings of Cambridge University.

There, in 1209 – the most important date in the whole of Cambridge's long calendar – riots involving townspeople and students resulted in three of the latter being hanged. Because of the violence, students from

Cambridge skyline at night

Oxford migrated across country to the small town of Cambridge on the edge of the vast fens.

Did they make the journey because they knew there was already a body of students waiting in Cambridge? Did they migrate because they knew there was already a body of learning within the walls of the ecclesiastical communities of Cambridge? We do not know, but came they certainly did, and now it is generally accepted that 1209 was the 'birthdate' of Cambridge University.

It is odd that twenty years later, scholars from the older University of Paris made a similar migration to Cambridge. Had Cambridge established a reputation in just twenty years? Or had that intellectual reputation existed long before? In 1226 there is reference to a chancellor, and in 1231 Henry III instructed his sheriff to punish 'contumacious scholars' by imprisonment or expulsion from the town although, it should be noted, only at the discretion of the Chancellor and Masters of the University.

Much of the obscurity surrounding the earliest days of the university is due to the townsfolk's riot of 1261, when university records were burned. Already the ordinary people of Cambridge were realising that they were hosts to a new and powerful 'lord' in the form of the university. The 1261 riot led to sixteen townsmen and twenty-eight scholars being tried by three of Henry III's judges. The outcome, as was to happen so often in the future, was heavily in favour of the university — all the townsmen were hanged while the scholars were granted the King's pardon! Friction between town and gown continued for centuries.

Nevertheless, it was the existence and continuing development of the colleges — the first, Peterhouse, was started in 1284 — and the university which was to turn Cambridge from a prosperous little East Anglian market town with a brisk river trade into an internationally respected intellectual community. This process was not always to the benefit of the town which, to its dismay, began to realise that the powers of the university were becoming, to say the least, onerous. The Chancellor's Court, for example, allowed the Chancellor to try all civil and criminal cases involving teachers, and the bias was soon apparent. As more colleges were built, land within the medieval town's boundaries became crowded, the town became increasingly unhealthy, with the King's Ditch and the river nothing more than open sewers. River trade declined in the fourteenth century, many traders abandoning the town because of increasingly high mortality rates. The plague was a frequent visitor. Cambridge was becoming a dangerous place in which to live.

Town and gown unease

Town and gown continued to live together uneasily. In 1381 an extension of the Peasants' Revolt reached Cambridge, and the mob once again burned records and documents of both university and the colleges after breaking into the University Church of Great St Mary. They forced the Chancellor and the heads of colleges to give up their privileges and to abide by the common law. But their revolt was put down, and the town's leading officials were summoned to Westminster, where they were chastised and the university's privileges restored.

Henceforth Cambridge's progress, socially and topographically, was to be controlled principally by the growth of the colleges. The fourteenth century saw the foundation of Michael House and King's Hall (both absorbed later into Trinity College), Clare, Pembroke, Gonville, Trinity Hall and Corpus Christi — the latter, uniquely in either Cambridge or Oxford, having been founded by townsfolk, members of the guilds of Corpus Christi and the Holy Virgin Mary.

All of these foundations took up large tracts of land in the town. But it was half way through the fifteenth century when the centre of Cambridge started to be altered dramatically and magnificently.

The young and pious King Henry VI began to accumulate land in the town in the 1440s. His early plans for a new college were modest. Happily for future generations, they became more grandiose. Although he did not live to see it finished, he laid the foundations for his college's chapel. Today, King's College Chapel is one of the wonders of the world, an inspiration to the millions of visitors from the world over who flock to marvel at its grandeur. We will look at the chapel in greater detail later.

With the acquisition of such a huge site in the town centre, the academic domination of the old market town continued apace, and the fifteenth century saw the establishment of Queens', St Catharine's and Jesus colleges. At the same time, artisans were leaving the town in numbers, forced out, complained the burgesses at the time, by the arrival of increasingly large numbers of academics.

King Henry VIII and the Reformation were very nearly the undoing of intellectual Cambridge. Two of the religious houses were dissolved and refounded as colleges. The King's zeal to abolish all religious houses almost involved the suppression of the colleges in Cambridge and Oxford. However, an appeal was made to Henry's sixth wife Katherine Parr which apparently succeeded because not only did Henry reprieve the colleges but established his own, Trinity, in 1546 shortly before he died.

River trade was neglected in the early sixteenth century but new prosperity was at hand. Corn became king and Cambridge a major centre for dealing in the commodity. The Reformation brought with it a thirst for learning, and printing and bookbinding formed an important part of the local economy as they do to this day. The Cambridge University Press goes back to 1534, when the university was given the right to license three printers. It is the world's oldest existing Bible printer and publisher, and today's Press, housed in fine modern buildings on the edge of the city, is recognised as one of the world's most prestigious publishing-houses.

Sanitation

Sanitation, as elsewhere, was appalling in Cambridge, and an effort to improve the water supply was made in 1610 with a new stream of fresh water being brought from springs to the south of the town into the very heart of the market square. The water flowed down runnels in Trumpington and St Andrew's streets; those in Trumpington Street still survive. This system provided drinking-water for Cambridge for 250 years. Called Hobson's Conduit, it was named after that remarkable son of Cambridge, Thomas Hobson, the carrier whose insistence on letting his horses out to clients in strict rotation gave us the saying 'Hobson's choice', meaning no choice at all.

The Civil War

Ancient rivalries and bitterness 'twixt town and gown were hugely emphasised during the Civil War. Oliver Cromwell, born 17 miles *27 km* away at Huntingdon, had come up as a student at Sidney Sussex College for a year in 1616, had been elected Member of Parliament for the town in 1640 and, recognising the strategic importance of Cambridge, made it his base for the Eastern Counties Association in the early days of the war. The town stood almost entirely for Cromwell, while the colleges were mainly royalist. Post-war Cambridge was uncomfortable!

The seventeenth century had seen the addition of Jesus, Christ's, St John's, Magdalene, Trinity and Emmanuel to the list of colleges. There was to be no new college until Downing in 1800. But the population increased rapidly in the seventeenth and eighteenth centuries without any expansion of the town's boundaries, resulting in an explosion of small, mean houses, crowded in upon each other.

Dr John Addenbrooke, of St Catharine's College, died in 1719, leaving £4,500 to found a hospital. 'Addenbrooke's' is now world-famous.

Improvement Commissioners were appointed later in the eighteenth century to improve lighting, cleansing and paving , the open fields outside the town were enclosed at the beginning of the nineteenth century, and suburban housing sprouted there. The railway arrived in 1845 — the university insisted the station should be well away from the colleges — and ruined the river trade.

Modern Cambridge

Girton, Newnham and Selwyn colleges were nineteenth-century foundations to be followed in the twentieth by New Hall, Churchill, Fitzwilliam and finally Robinson. But it was the nineteenth century which brought most benefits to town and gown. Political reforms meant increased enfranchisement and a properly elected town council, most of the university privileges which had infuriated the citizenry for so long were abolished, the university expanded, hugely affecting the town's topography with new lecture-rooms and laboratories, and college Fellows, finally allowed to marry in 1882, built many fine family houses.

Thus the town had at last broken free from its medieval boundaries, and its suburbs began to reach out towards the necklace villages so that Cambridge was ready to assume its twentieth-century role as a city of international importance.

Later pages will look more closely at the facilities which the city has to offer to citizen and visitor alike. Now it is sufficient to keep in one's mind's eye a picture of Cambridge as a city of remarkable contrasts — narrow streets and enclosed courts surrounded by open commons and public parks, the medieval magnificence of great colleges mingling with buildings housing the very latest in technological advances, tradition couched comfortably with innovation, town and gown happily integrated at last – and a tranquil river flowing past a small hill upon which the Norman castle mound still stands.

Modern architecture

The international reputation of the glories of Cambridge's traditional architecture should not deter the visitor from enjoying the splendours of its modern and contemporary buildings.

Cambridge was influenced early – domestically, at least – by the Modern Movement. Indeed, one of the earliest of Modern buildings in England, the 'prism pure' White House in Conduit Head Road, was designed by George Checkley in 1931.

It was to be the traditionalist colleges, however, which were to embrace warmly the new architectural philosophy. Gonville and Caius College's South Range, opposite the Guildhall and overlooking the Market Square, was the first modern building in the city centre (Murray Easton, 1934). At Peterhouse, the oldest college, modern Fen Court was designed in 1939 by Hughes & Bicknell.

Little changed until the 1950s, when two new colleges were built in the Modern manner, Fitzwilliam (designed by Sir Denys Lasdun in 1958, built in the 1960s) and Churchill (Richard Sheppard, Robson & Partners, designed 1958–9 and built 1959–68). At Queens' College, Sir Basil Spence designed the Erasmus Building (1960) – the first Modern building on the Backs. It aroused considerable controversy.

The 1960s and 1970s saw hugely increased building programmes mostly in the Modern style. Among the new buildings: the William Stone building at Peterhouse (Sir Leslie Martin and Colin St John Wilson, 1963–4), New Hall, a brand-new college for women (Chamberlain Powell & Bon, 1962–6), the Master's Lodge, Emmanuel College (Tom Hancock, 1963–4), the George Thomson Building, Corpus Christi College (Philip Dawson, Arup Associates, 1963–4), the Cripps Building, St John's College (Powell & Moya, 1962–7) and New Court, Christ's College (Sir Denys Lasdun & Partners, 1966–70), the highly contro-versial Faculty of History Building (James Stirling, 1964–8), the Wolfson Building, Trinity College (Architects Co-Partnership, 1968–72), Science Laboratories, New Museums Site (Arup Associates, 1971), Cripps Court, Queens' College (Powell & Moya, 1972–9), the Faculty of Music (Sir Leslie Martin, Colin Lumley, Ivor Richards, 1975–80) and Cambridge's newest college and the only one designed for both men and women students, Robinson (Gillespie, Kidd & Coia, 1977–81).

The two most spectacular modern industrial buildings in Cambridge are undoubtedly the Napp Laboratories on the Cambridge Science Park in Milton Road (Arthur Erickson, 1981–3) and the Schlum-berger Building in the west of the city off Madingley Road (Michael Hopkins, 1984–5).

Schlumberger Research Institute at night

Napp Laboratories

In the 1990s several colleges, among them Darwin, St John's, Jesus and Trinity Hall, built much-needed new libraries, and a gift of £10m from the A.P. Møller and Chastine Mc-Kinney Møller Foundation, a Danish institution, to Churchill College resulted in the building there in 1992 of the Møller Centre for Continuing Education. The building, designed by Danish architect Henning Larsen, was opened by Queen Ingrid of Denmark. The University's exciting new Law Faculty Building, designed by Sir Norman Foster and Partners, brought the scattered Faculty buildings under one roof for the first time in the 600 years that law has been taught at Cambridge.

As the old millennium died, the former Addenbrooke's Hospital in Trumpington Street was re-created as the Judge Institute of Management Studies, and the Isaac Newton Institute for Mathematical Sciences was born in Clarkson Road. Now the largest building scheme ever undertaken by the university is exploding on the 60ha West Cambridge development site – a 20-year capital programme of more than £400m.

Famous names

Detail from a copy of a portrait of Oliver Cromwell by Peter Lely

To list the names of all the famous people connected with Cambridge down the centuries would be far beyond the scope of this guide. Thirteen British prime ministers, for example, were Cambridge men, including the first, Sir Robert Walpole, the youngest, William Pitt, and the only one to be assassinated, Spencer Perceval, who was shot in the lobby of the House of Commons in 1812. For centuries not only the State but the Church – nine archbishops of Canterbury – and the Law have been influenced by those with a Cambridge background.

Eighty Nobel prize-winners – thirty-one from Trinity College – have had strong Cambridge connections. Virtually every area of human endeavour has been touched by those educated at Cambridge – from martyrdom (**Thomas Cranmer**, **Nicholas Ridley** and **Hugh Latimer** were burned at the stake in Oxford in the reign of Mary Tudor) to espionage (**Guy Burgess**, **Donald Maclean**, **Anthony Blunt** and **Kim Philby** spied for the Soviet Union).

Undoubtedly the greatest of the Cambridge 'greats' was **Sir Isaac Newton**, of Trinity College. It has been said that if, in its nearly 800-year history, Cambridge had only produced Newton that would have been sufficient justification for the university's existence because without Newton's genius the twentieth century as we know it today would not exist.

Here, then, follows a necessarily restricted selection of distinguished people past and present with Cambridge connections. It is dominated by men because women students did not arrive in Cambridge until 1873.

Among royalty and statesmen are **King Edward VII**, **Queen Margarethe of Denmark**, **Charles, Prince of Wales**, and **HRH Prince Edward**; **Oliver Cromwell**, a local man who came up to his Cambridge college, Sidney Sussex, on 23 April 1616, the very day of Shakespeare's death, stayed for just a year due to the death of his father but went on to sit for Cambridge in the Short and Long Parliaments, signed Charles I's death warrant and finally took supreme power in the State as the Lord Protector; **Lord Mountbatten**, who presided over the transfer of power from Britain to India as the last Viceroy; **Jawaharlal Nehru**, Mountbatten's friend, who became first Prime Minister of India after independence; **Rajiv Gandhi**, a later Prime Minister of India, who was assassinated, and **Lee Kuan Yew**, a Prime Minister of Singapore.

Poets, dramatists and writers include **Lord Byron** and **Alfred, Lord Tennyson**; **William Wordsworth**, who wrote of his Cambridge life in 'The Prelude'; **Samuel Taylor Coleridge**; **John Milton** of Christ's College, whose only extant manuscript is, oddly, in Trinity College's Wren Library; **Thomas Gray** ('Elegy Written in a Country Churchyard'); **Edmund Spenser**; **Robert**

Isaac Newton, Trinity College Chapel

King Edward VII

Herrick ('Gather ye rosebuds while ye may'); **Christopher Marlowe**, the dramatist stabbed to death in a brawl aged twenty-nine and fellow Elizabethan **John Fletcher**; **Francis Bacon**; **Samuel Pepys**, whose entire library graces his college, Magdalene; **John Dryden**; **Charles Kingsley** (*The Water Babies*); **William Makepeace Thackeray**; **A.E. Housman**; **A.A. Milne** (his son, **Christopher Robin**, followed him to Trinity College as a student); First World War poets **Rupert Brooke** and **Siegfried Sassoon**; **E.M. Forster**; **Christopher Isherwood**; **J.B. Priestley**; **C.P. (Lord) Snow**, both novelist and physicist; **Sylvia Plath** and **Tom Sharpe**.

The list of eminent scientists, mathematicians, astronomers, philosophers and medical practitioners is immense. Scientists at the Cavendish Laboratory alone have won more than twenty-five Nobel prizes.

William Harvey discovered the circulation of the blood; **Professor Sir Roy Calne** and **Sir Terence English** are among the world's leading transplant surgeons; **Charles Darwin** discovered natural selection; **Desiderius Erasmus** brought the teaching of Greek to the university and later prepared men's minds for the Reformation; **Lord Rutherford** led the 1930s team which first split the atom; **Charles Babbage** built the first calculating-machine; **Sir Frank Whittle** developed the jet engine; **Francis Crick** and **James Watson** unravelled the structure of the DNA molecule; **Professor Sir Martin Ryle** used radio astronomy to study galaxies and stars in space; **Bertrand Russell** was one of the great logicians and **Ludwig Wittgenstein** was long the dominating philosophical figure of the English-speaking world. Today, **Professor Stephen Hawking**'s startling mathematical thinking has brought him international acclaim.

Cambridge personalities are found throughout the worlds of theatre, journalism and broadcasting. Actress

HRH Charles, the Prince of Wales

Sir Jack Hobbs

made the names of cricket and Cambridge indivisible, the incomparable **Sir Jack Hobbs**.

And among many other famous Cambridge people **Matthew Parker**, Master of Corpus Christi College and second Protestant Archbishop of Canterbury, whose long nose and inquiring mind gave us the expression 'Nosey Parker'; **Thomas Gresham**, founder of the Royal Exchange (forerunner of the Stock Exchange); **William Wilberforce** who helped to end the slave trade; **John Harvard**, founder of Harvard University; **Paul Mellon**, American collector, philanthropist and racehorse-owner, and **Thomas Hobson**, the Cambridge carrier who insisted his customers hired his horses in strict rotation thus giving us 'Hobson's choice', which means no choice at all. ☐

Emma Thompson; composer **Ralph Vaughan Williams**; broadcasters **Sir Alastair Cooke, Sir David Frost, Bamber Gascoigne, Clive James**; actors **Sir Ian McKellen, Sir Derek Jacobi, John Cleese, Peter Cook, Tim Brooke-Taylor**; journalists **Katharine Whitehorn, Joan Bakewell** and **Germaine Greer**.

Both city and university have long excelled in sport of all kinds and have produced Olympic athletes like **Lord Burghley** and **Harold Abrahams**, international rugby-players (more than 300 Cambridge University players have been capped by their country) like **Micky Steele-Bodger, Rob Andrew** (capped more than fifty times for England), and Cambridgeshire-born **Dickie Jeeps**; international and Olympic oarsmen such as **Edward Bevan, James Crowden** (now Lord Lieutenant for Cambridgeshire) and **Ian Watson**; cricketing stars such as **Mike Atherton, Peter May, Mike Brearley, Ranjit Singh** and, of course, the man who

Emma Thompson

City walks

*Trinity College
Great Gate*

ambridge, a small and compact city, is ideal to walk round, and this is the best way to appreciate its splendid buildings and delightful open spaces – but please remember that the colleges are private places of study. Visit them quietly! They do not permit dogs, and you are asked not to eat or drink in the college grounds. Please do not walk on the grass – this is a privilege reserved for senior members of each college.

Some colleges charge admission, and some, when open, are open to visitors only at certain times of the day. Most colleges are closed to visitors during the examination period – from mid April to mid June. King's College Chapel generally remains open. Groups of ten or more wanting to go into the colleges must be accompanied by a Cambridge Blue Badge Guide, who can be booked through the Tourist Information Centre.

Before you set off on your walk may we suggest you check with the Tourist Information Centre about college opening times, admission charges, etc. All the walks start at the Tourist Information Centre, but they are all circular walks and can thus be joined anywhere *en route*.

Walks 1 and 2 are for when the colleges are open, and Walks 3 and 4 when they are closed, the latter visiting the Backs.

Walk 1

This walk is for when the colleges are open. It will take you into the main riverside colleges and is the obvious choice if this is your first visit to Cambridge. If you have never been to Cambridge before, this is the ideal introduction for the walk will take you into Corpus Christi, King's, Clare, Trinity Hall, Trinity and St John's colleges and through some of the ancient, narrow lanes as well as past some of the city's varied and fine shops. Allow about 2½ hours.

Turn right outside the **Tourist Information Centre**. Look right along **Peas Hill**, the medieval fish market and nothing like a 'hill'. Medieval Cambridge was low-lying,

and this was above the marshy ground. 'Peas' is thought to come from *piscaria*, Latin for 'fish market'. There are enormous cellars under the road that were used as air-raid shelters during the Second World War. The Cambridge University Footlights stage their annual revue at the **Arts Theatre**.

Left into **Bene't** (short for Benedict) **Street**. At the medieval **Friars' House** look left up **Free School Lane**. There is the old **Cavendish Laboratory** (1847), one of the most famous laboratories in the world. In 1932 Ernest Rutherford led the team which split the atom for the first time, and in the 1950s Francis Crick and James Watson discovered the structure of DNA here. Turn round. Under roof guttering of No. 5 are three iron rings. If medieval timber buildings caught fire, hooks put in the rings were used to pull off the thatched roof to prevent the fire spreading.

Friars' House

See main map on pages 6–7 for general key

| 0 | 100 | 200 Metres |

| 0 | 100 | 200 Yards |

Start point

⟷ Walk route

WC Toilet

The tower of **St Bene't's Church** on the left, with its Saxon long and short corner-stones, is the oldest building in the county, about 1025. The round holes above the double-belfry windows were used by nesting owls, which devoured the church mice! The churchyard is at medieval ground level. Streets were artificially raised above the floodline. Inside the church on your right is one of the old fire-hooks and a seventeenth-century coffin-stool. Fabian Stedman, parish clerk in 1670, invented change-ringing. The first organised peal of bells was probably rung from here. In the case in the right-hand corner is Thomas Hobson's Bible. He owned a livery stable and insisted his customers hired the horse nearest the door because that had rested longest. Hence the expression 'Hobson's choice' — no choice. This church was used by Corpus Christi College until they built their own chapel.

Cross the road under the carriage-arch into the courtyard of **the Eagle**, a former coaching-inn. Call in for a drink later and look at the ceiling in the Air Force Bar, where US and Allied airmen burned their squadron names and numbers with candles and cigarette-lighters during the Second World War.

At the end of Bene't Street, turn left. The modern buildings across the road on the right are on the site of Hobson's stables. The college on the right is **St Catharine's** (1473) with her gilded Catharine wheel in the wrought-iron gate. William Wotton of St Catharine's was the youngest under-graduate ever to come to Cambridge University. Born 1666, he knew Latin, Greek and Hebrew at the age of six and came to Cambridge aged nine.

Up the steps on the left into **Corpus**

Corpus Christi College

Christi College. The neo-Gothic **New Court** was designed in the 1820s. The door to the **chapel** is immediately opposite you, but please remember not to walk on the grass! The range on your right is the college **library**, left many books and manuscripts by Matthew Parker, Master in 1544 and Archbishop of Canterbury in Elizabeth I's reign. He had a long nose and an inquiring mind and was always asking questions — the original 'Nosey Parker'. Go left round the court to the far left archway, down the steps into the **Old Court**, the oldest in Cambridge, built soon after the foundation in 1352. Notice the old doorways and windows; there was no glass originally — oiled linen kept out the cold east winds. There was no heating, and students slept on rushes on the floor. Go left around the court to the memorial to Christopher Marlowe and John Fletcher, both students here. Turn round; diagonally across the court the old **Master's Lodge** has the college emblem, a pelican, carved above the door. Tradition says that during famines a pelican mother pecks her breast and feeds her young on her blood. Leave through what was the original entrance,

King's Parade

noting the tiny door on the left, marked 'Bedmakers Only'. People were smaller in the Middle Ages.

Turn left, then right along **King's Parade** with its splendidly varied range of buildings. On the left, is the nineteenth-century stone screen and gatehouse of **King's College** (1441). Right of the gateway is a nine-teenth-century hexagonal post-box with 'VR' — *Victoria Regina*. If the gate is open, go into the college (turn to p. 94 to read about King's College and Chapel). If it is not, continue along King's Parade, and we will enter the chapel by the north door later.

The last shop on the right is Ryder & Amies, university outfitters. In its windows are the university sporting fixture lists, showing which students have been chosen for the various university teams.

Great St Mary's, the University Church, is late Gothic Perpendicular, built between 1478 and 1519. The 114-foot 35-m high tower, finished later, is often open to the public. Climb the 123 steps to the top for spectacular views of the city and colleges. Until 1730, degrees were awarded here. The University Sermons are still preached here each term. A curfew bell was rung every night at 9 o'clock, after which all students had to be back in college. The quarter chimes on the 1793 clock were subsequently copied for Big Ben at West-minster and are now called 'Westminster chimes' — but Cambridge had them first! At the base of the tower the ring cut in the right-hand side is a datum point. This is the centre of Cambridge from which all distances are measured.

The corner bookshop beyond the church now belongs to the Cambridge University Press. This is the site of the oldest book-shop in Britain. Books have been sold here since 1581.

Across the road from Great St Mary's is the heart of Cambridge University. Facing you is the **Old Schools**, standing on the first land bought by the university. Behind the eighteenth-century classical façade are the oldest university buildings in Cambridge, built in the late fourteenth century. End on to the road is the elegant **Senate House** (1730) designed by James Gibbs. Here the Council of the Senate, the governing body of the university, meets, students wearing their gowns come here to be awarded their degrees, and honorary degrees are given here annually. Examination results are posted on wooden boards beneath the Senate House windows. In 1958 engineering students raised a small car onto the Senate House roof overnight. It took the authorities nearly a week to get it down.

Turn left into **Senate House Passage**. The splendid gate on the right is the Gate of Honour of **Gonville and Caius College**. Dr Caius (pronounced 'Keys') refounded the college in 1557 with three gates symbolising a student's academic life. The student entered through the Gate of Humility, passed under the Gate of Virtue and finally through the Gate of Honour to receive his degree.

Turn and look back up Senate House Passage. The gap between the small, dark turret of Gonville and Caius on the left and the far end of the Senate House roof on the right is the 'Senate House Leap', traditionally jumped by members of the unofficial 'Night Climbers' Club'.

At the bottom of the passage, bear left. The large gateway on your left, which now leads to the university's administrative offices, was the original gatehouse of King's College Old Court. You are walking on one of the main streets in the city before Henry VI built his college across it.

Ahead is the entrance to **King's College** and **Chapel**. If you wish to enter the college, please turn to p. 94. To continue the walk after your visit, leave King's by this same gate.

On the left, **Clare College** (1326), the second oldest Cambridge College, founded by a chancellor of the university and refounded twelve years later by Lady Elizabeth de Clare. Her lozenge on the wrought-iron gate is encircled by a black mourning-band with gold tear-drops. Poor Lady Elizabeth was always crying – she had three husbands, and they all died before she was thirty. Walk through the college. The original buildings became so decrepit that they were rebuilt in the seventeenth century. The Civil War disrupted building work, and the court took seventy-seven years to complete. **Clare Bridge** (1639) is the oldest bridge still standing on the river. How many stone balls does it have on the balustrade? Fourteen? Look again. The next but last on the left has a slice cut out of the back. The architect was paid the equivalent of 15p for his design, so the story goes. Feeling hard done by, he vowed the bridge would never be completed ...

All the land behind six of the riverside colleges on the far side of the Cam is called

Clare College Bridge balustrade

the **Backs** — it used to be Backsides. On Clare Backs the beautiful **Fellows' Garden** is often open to the public; and here you can walk on the grass! Return to the college entrance and turn left.

The next college on the left is **Trinity Hall**, founded in 1350 to help counter the ravages of the Black Death among lawyers and churchmen — Trinity Hall is traditionally known as the lawyers' college. If the college is open, please go in. **Principal Court** was built in the late fourteenth century but refaced in the eighteenth century. Look for a tiny original casement in the far right corner of the court. The coat of arms on the right shows the college was founded by a bishop. Continue through the doors ahead, with the **dining-hall** on the left, to see the Elizabethan **library**, built with thin Tudor bricks, on the right. Inside upstairs are original Jacobean reading-desks with some

Trinity Hall old library

books still chained to prevent their removal. The small door high in the wall was once used by the Master, who had a walkway from his lodge opposite. Do look at the crow-stepped gable end of this old building before retracing your steps back through the college.

Turn left outside the college, then right along **Trinity Lane**. The gate on your left may be open for a view of **Trinity College Great Court**.

Continue up the lane and turn left into **Trinity Street**, walking past excellent shops with fine façades. Hobbs sports shop on the left was started by Sidney, brother of the famous cricketer, Sir Jack Hobbs. On the right, Laura Ashley's was once an inn called the Turk's Head, where the wealthy and aristocratic undergraduate members of 'The True Blue and Beefsteak Club' used to eat gargantuan dinners washed down by gallons of wine. The Blue Boar on the right was a coaching-inn, and Heffers Children's Bookshop on the left has a superb late-1700s shop-front.

Turn left onto the cobbles outside the **Great Gate** of **Trinity College**, founded in 1546 by Henry VIII as one of the last acts of his life — he died six weeks later. Henry's statue is on the gate. In his left hand is the golden orb. What is in his right? A chair-leg! It was put there by students who removed the golden sceptre many years ago.

The shields and coats of arms are those of Edward III – who founded an earlier college on the site – and his six sons. The blank shield was for William of Hatfield who died in infancy. Look right. The small tree in the middle of the lawn, planted in the 1950s, is a descendant of the apple-tree under which Isaac Newton was sitting at his home in Woolsthorpe, Lincolnshire, when,

Wren Library, Trinity College

according to tradition, an apple hitting him on the head led him to discover the laws of gravity. Newton came up to Trinity in 1661. His rooms were to the right of the Great Gate. Trinity College has produced thirty-one Nobel prize-winners.

Enter **Trinity Great Court**, the largest in either Oxford or Cambridge, covering over 2 acres *0.8 ha*. Ahead is the ivy-covered **Master's Lodge**. Most colleges choose their own Master, but the Master of Trinity is always chosen by the reigning monarch. It was Master Thomas Nevile, chosen by Elizabeth I, who created this magnificent court. On your right is **Edward III's Gate**. Edward holds a sword with three crowns to show he considered himself king of England, France and Scotland. The large clock above him has a double strike, low note then high; William Wordsworth calls it the clock with a 'male and female voice'. While it is striking 12 o'clock (i.e. twenty-four times), students try to run round the Great Court — 380 yards *347.5 m* in 43 seconds. Only the late Marquis of Exeter has succeeded. The run was featured in the film *Chariots of Fire*, but Harold Abrahams never attempted it, and the sequence was not filmed here.

If it is open, go through the doorway on the right of Edward III's gate into the college **chapel** started by Mary Tudor in 1554. The ante-chapel has statues of famous Trinity men; that of Isaac Newton holding a prism is said to be the finest statue in Cambridge. Engraved on the wall behind him are the names of Trinity men killed in the Second World War. There is a statue of Alfred, Lord Tennyson, his beloved tobacco-pipe half-hidden under laurel leaves on his right and of Francis Bacon, philosopher, lawyer and essayist, who wrote mainly in Latin; he was not sure the English language would survive. The chapel was panelled in the eighteenth century, and the altarpiece by Benjamin West shows St Michael killing the devil.

Return to the Great Court and walk towards the fountain in which poet Lord Byron reputedly swam when an undergraduate. Students were not allowed to keep dogs in college (they are still not). So Byron bought a bear and kept it in an attic in the tower in the far left-hand corner. On your right is the **dining-hall** (1604). The roof lantern shows where smoke from the brazier in the hall could escape. If there is no notice to the contrary, go up the steps, through the dining-hall screen, to see cloistered **Nevile's Court** (1612). Ahead of you is the **Wren Library** (1695), designed for no fee by Sir Christopher Wren . The roof statues represent Divinity, Law, Physic and Mathematics. The library is generally open to the public from Monday to Friday 1200–1400, Saturdays in full term 1030–1230. It has 55,000 books printed before 1820 and 2,500 volumes of manuscripts. One modern manuscript is that of *Winnie the Pooh* – A.A. Milne and his son Christopher Robin were Trinity men.

Retrace your steps to the Great Gate. Turn left. The next gate-tower leads into **St John's College** (1511). Above the gate St John's statue has his emblem, the eagle, at his feet. The coat of arms of the found-ress, Lady Margaret Beaufort, is supported by mythical yales, with goats' heads, antelopes' bodies and elephants' tails. Their horns move independently. There are daisies (marguerites) and forget-me-nots, symbolising her motto *Souvent me Souvient*. Can you spot a fox entering its lair above the nose of the yale on the right?

Ahead and above you in **First Court** is a statue of the foundress. To your right are the stone foundations of the first chapel, behind which is the college's Victorian **chapel**. At noon on Ascension Day, the college choir sings hymns from the top of the chapel tower.

Go into the chapel. The ante-chapel has the tomb of Hugh Ashton lying in academic robes but underneath he is an emaciated, shrouded corpse. There is a statue to William Wilberforce who helped abolish slavery. The huge west window shows the Day of Judgement — in the bottom right of which sinners are being pushed into the fiery furnace.

Proceed to **Second Court**. The statue ahead is of Mary, Countess of Shrewsbury, who paid for most of this court. On the right the oriel window is in the longest room in Cambridge. The senior combination room is 93 feet *28.3 m* long and still lit only by candlelight. Plans for the D-Day landings in Europe were drawn up here.

In **Third Court**, bear left under the arch.

Bridge of Sighs, St John's College

Stand on Kitchen Bridge and look right at the **Bridge of Sighs** (1831), built to join **New Court** to the old college. One night students punted a mini-car upriver and suspended it by rope under the bridge. The beautiful Gothic Revival New Court, built in the 1820s, was promptly nicknamed 'The Wedding Cake'.

Retrace your steps to the street. Turn left. At the corner, look left along **Bridge Street** at the fine range of restored medieval buildings. Ahead is the **Church of the Holy Sepulchre**, one of four surviving 'round' churches in England. Its round nave and aisle were built in the first half of the twelfth century. Eight massive Norman pillars have slender double Norman arches above them. The east window (1946) shows Christ crucified on a living tree — the Tree of Life; it replaces a Victorian window blown out by a wartime bomb. The church was extensively restored in the 1840s.

Leaving the church, turn left . A footpath leads to the famous **Cambridge Union Society** where many leading politicians began their careers in the Debating Chamber.

Walk on into **Sidney Street**, where **Sidney Sussex College** (1596) is on your left. Enter **Chapel Court** on the right through the gateway. Oliver Cromwell was an undergraduate here, and in 1960 his skull was buried secretly under the antechapel floor.

Continue along Sidney Street. In the nineteenth century the street was full of elegant houses and shops. The 1920s saw huge demolition, and many old businesses disappeared. Look left down **Sussex Street**. The modern, high-level covered bridge links two parts of Sidney Sussex College.

Bridge Street

Turn right into **Market Street**, one of the city's oldest shopping streets. In 1592 it was called Shoemakers' Lane. **Holy Trinity Church** is on your left. The original twelfth-century building was destroyed in the great fire of 1174. Rebuilding began in the fourteenth century. Charles Simeon, of the evangelical movement, was minister here from 1782 to 1836. He was one of the first people to use an umbrella. That and his teapot are in the vestry.

Continue into **Market Hill**. The medieval guildhall stood here and the prison with its stocks and pillory — rotten fruit and vegetables were always available to be thrown at criminals. The excellent market is open every day with a great variety of stalls. On the front of the large, modern **Guildhall** (1937) is the city's coat of arms with the river and the all-important bridge. Behind the Guildhall is the **Tourist Information Centre** — and we are back where we started. □

Walk 2

This walk is for when the colleges are open but covers the southern area of the city, going through Queens' College to the Mill Pool and on through Pembroke, Emmanuel and Christ's colleges before returning to the city centre. Allow 2 to 2½ hours.

Turn right outside the **Tourist Information Centre**. Look right along **Peas Hill**, the medieval fish market and nothing like a 'hill'. Medieval Cambridge was low-lying, and this was above the marshy ground. 'Peas' is thought to come from *piscaria*, Latin for 'fish market'. There are enormous cellars under the road that were used as air-raid shelters during the Second World War. The Cambridge University Footlights stage their annual revue at the **Arts Theatre**.

Left into **Bene't** (short for Benedict) **Street**. At the medieval **Friars' House** look left up **Free School Lane**. There is the old **Cavendish Laboratory** (1847), one of the most famous laboratories in the world. In 1932 Ernest Rutherford led the team which split the atom for the first time, and in the 1950s the structure of DNA was discovered here by Francis Crick and James Watson. Turn round. Under roof guttering of No. 5 are three iron rings. If medieval timber buildings caught fire, hooks put in the rings were used to pull off the thatched roof to prevent the fire spreading.

The tower of **St Bene't's Church** on the left, with its Saxon long and short cornerstones, is the oldest building in the county, about 1025. The round holes above the double-belfry windows were used by nesting owls, which devoured the church mice!

The churchyard is at medieval ground level. Streets were artificially raised above the floodline. Inside the church on your right is one of the old fire-hooks and a seventeenth-century coffin-stool. Fabian Stedman, parish clerk in 1670, invented change-ringing. The first organised peal of bells was probably rung from here. In the case in the south-west corner is Thomas Hobson's Bible. He owned a livery stable and insisted his customers hired the horse nearest the door because that had rested longest. Hence the expression 'Hobson's choice' — no choice. This church was used by Corpus Christi College until they built their own chapel.

St Catharine's College gate

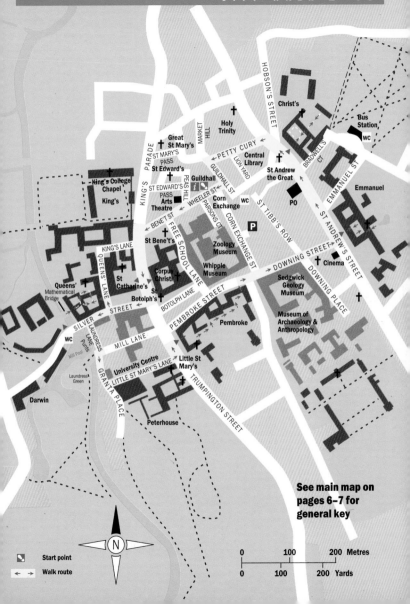

See main map on pages 6–7 for general key

0   100   200 Metres

0   100   200 Yards

◩ Start point

← → Walk route

Cross the road under the carriage-arch into the courtyard of **the Eagle**, a former coaching-inn. Call in for a drink later and look at the ceiling in the Air Force Bar, where US and Allied airmen burned their names, squadron names and numbers with candles and cigarette lighters during the Second World War.

At the end of Bene't Street, turn left. The modern buildings across the road on the right are on the site of Hobson's stables. The college on the right is **St Catharine's** (1473) with her gilded Catharine wheel in the wrought-iron gate. William Wotton of St Catharine's was the youngest under-graduate ever to come to Cambridge University. Born 1666, he knew Latin, Greek and Hebrew at the age of six and came to Cambridge aged nine.

On your left, **Corpus Christi College** (1352). Through the gate you get a glimpse of the **New Court**. The **chapel** door immediately opposite has statues either side. On the right is Matthew Parker, college Master in 1544 and Archbishop of Canterbury in the reign of Elizabeth I. A brilliant man who was always asking questions — from him we get the expression 'Nosey Parker'.

Next is **St Botolph's Church** (1320). Botolph was a seventh-century Saxon saint who became the patron saint of travellers. His churches were tradi-tionally built beside city gates, where you prayed for a good journey and gave thanks for a safe return.

Cross the road from St Botolph's to Ede & Ravenscroft, who have been making academic robes since 1689. They hold the four royal warrants

Ede & Ravenscroft – academic robes

Queens' College sundial and moondial

in 1465 hence the plural spelling of 'Queens' College'. But the original founder, Andrew Dokett, has his likeness carved over the entrance gate. Go through the gate into **Old Court**, the best preserved medieval court in Cambridge. The dial of 1733 is one of the finest examples of a sundial in Britain and one of the few moondials in the world. Walk ahead through the **screens passage**. On your right is the original **dining-hall**, classicised in the eighteenth century and returned to its medieval state in the nineteenth. A portrait of Elizabeth of Woodville hangs above the high table where the senior members sit, on her right is a portrait of Desiderius Erasmus. There are William Morris tiles in the fireplace.

Continue through the passage, turning right. The half-timbered sixteenth-century long gallery is built on fifteenth-century cloisters. Opposite the gallery in the corner is **Erasmus's Tower**. He lived here from 1510 to 1514. He had many complaints about Cambridge — our wine was like vinegar, the beer even worse, his expenses were enormous and his profits not a brass farthing. But he did think the women of Cambridge were nice to kiss!

On through the passage ahead to cross the famous **Mathematical Bridge** over the **River Cam**, looking carefully at the way the bridge is constructed. The story was that the original bridge (1749) had no nails to hold it together, the students took it down and the college could not put it together again so they used bolts. Sadly this is untrue. The present bridge of 1905 was built to the original design which had bolts at the main joints.

Return to **Cloister Court**, under the arch in the far left-hand corner, to **Walnut Tree Court**, where there are buildings from six

of the British royal family. They have made the coronation robes of every sovereign since William III. Look left across **Silver Street** to the church-like **Pitt Building**, named after William Pitt the Younger and part of the Cambridge University Press. Cambridge became the first university to have its own printing-press when Henry VIII gave them a royal warrant in 1534.

Walk down Silver Street. On your left, the university **Department of Applied Mathematics and Theoretical Physics**. Turn right into **Queens' Lane**. **Queens' College** was refounded by two queens, Margaret of Anjou, wife of Henry VI, in 1448 and Elizabeth of Woodville, wife of Edward IV, different centuries. Walk through the small passage on your right, back into Old Court and leave the college as you entered, returning to Silver Street. Cross over to go down **Laundress Lane** to the **Mill Pool**. For centuries a scene of frantic commercial activity, today this part of the river is reserved for punts, rowing-boats and canoes. You can pole your own hired punt or have a 'chauffeur'.

Across the river is **Laundress Green** where the laundry-women once spread their washing out to dry. The Old Granary opposite was the home of Charles Darwin's eldest son. Since 1964 it has been part of **Darwin College** (1964), the first graduate college in the university.

Walk past the **Cambridge University Centre**, the modern building on your left (1967). Ahead is the prestigious **Garden House Moat House Hotel**. Turn left into **Little St Mary's Lane** with its attractive sixteenth-, seventeenth- and eighteenth-century cottages. Notice the inn sign of the old Half Moon pub and the original gas street lights which burn constantly. The churchyard is maintained as a wild garden by residents of the lane.

The first church on this site, St Peter-without-Trumpington-Gate was used by the next-door college, which took the name **Peterhouse**. In the fourteenth century the church was rebuilt and renamed the **Church of St Mary the Less** or Little St Mary's as it is affectionately called. Inside the church on your left is a memorial to Godfrey Washington, 'Minister of this Church and Fellow of St Peter's College', great-uncle of George Washington. Notice the family coat of arms, said to have inspired the flag of the United States — the Stars and Stripes. The font is thought to

have been a gift of Mathew Wren, uncle of Christopher.

Turn right on the path, then right again onto the lawn at the west end of the church. Look up at the left-hand window on the top floor of the building ahead of you, part of Peterhouse. Outside is a metal bar placed there for a fire escape by the poet Thomas Gray ('Elegy Written in a Country Church-yard') in 1756. When unsympathetic students pretended there was a fire he was so upset he left Peterhouse and moved to Pembroke College.

Notice the channels either side of **Trumpington Street**. They are often full of water and are part of an early seventeenth-century plan to bring fresh water into the city. Carrier Thomas Hobson gave money for this project, and the runnels are still called **Hobson's Conduit**.

Over the road is the west end of **Pembroke College Chapel**, the first building completed by Christopher Wren. Cross the road, walking left to the main entrance of Pembroke, founded in 1347 by Marie de St Pol de Valence, the widowed Countess of Pembroke. Aged seventeen, she married the fifty-year-old earl; legend says she was 'maid, wife and widow' all in one day, her husband being killed in front of her while jousting on their wedding-day.

Enter Pembroke under the old gateway into what was the smallest court of any college. Pemboke was the first college to have a private chapel. Follow the path to the right, entering their 'new' chapel. Christopher Wren's uncle, Mathew, Bishop of Ely, was imprisoned in the Tower of London for eighteen years by Oliver Cromwell. He vowed that if he was released safely he would build a chapel in his old college. Naturally, he asked his nephew to

Pembroke College Chapel
from Trumpington Street

design it. It was consecrated in 1665. Above the altar is a *Deposition* after Barocci. On its right is the chair of martyred Bishop Nicholas Ridley.

Outside, turn right up the steps, passing William Pitt's statue. He came up to Cambridge aged fourteen, became Chancellor of the Exchequer aged twenty-two and Prime Minister at twenty-four. The Victorian **dining-hall** is immediately on your left. Continue through the lovely gardens to the gate at the far left-hand corner and turn right up **Downing Street**, named after the same family which built Downing Street in London. We also have a 'No. 10, Downing Street'. To the right and left are university departments, laboratories and lecture halls.

Ahead of you is **Emmanuel College**, the first Protestant college. When it was founded in 1584 it was outside the city. Go through the classical entrance into **Front Court**. The Cloister Gallery and **chapel** facing you were all designed by Christopher Wren. Walk round the court to the right and through into the **Paddock** to the pond. You may walk on the grass near the pond! This site was a Dominican friary and the pond the monks' fishpond.

Turn round and look at the red brick building ahead on your left. It is thought that John Harvard lived here as an undergraduate. Harvard sailed to New England where he died of consumption in 1638, leaving money and his library of 320 books to found a 'schoale at Newetowne' which was called after him and became America's first university. One-third of the first 100 British university graduates to settle in New England were from Emmanuel College in Cambridge.

Enter the **chapel** through the small door left of the main one. Inside on the right is a plaque in Harvard's memory, given by the Harvard Society of America. The altar painting shows the return of the prodigal son by Jacopo Amigoni. The nineteenth-century stained glass windows include one of John Harvard but, as no one had a likeness of him, the head is reputedly that of the poet John Milton, a Cambridge contemporary of Harvard's. Continue round the court, keeping to the right. The **dining-hall** on your right was converted from the friars' chapel. Above the high table is a portrait of the college founder, Sir Walter Mildmay.

John Harvard (left), *Emmanuel College Chapel*

Master's Lodge, Christ's College

Leaving Emmanuel, turn right into **St Andrew's Street**, crossing Emmanuel Street and continuing until you reach **Christ's College** on your right. The church on your left is **St Andrew the Great** (1842). Inside is a monument to Captain James Cook, the navigator, who was murdered in Hawaii in 1779 and six of his children, three of whom died in infancy, one died as an undergraduate at Christ's College and two others died at sea. Mrs Cook and their two elder boys are buried in the middle aisle.

Christ's College was founded in 1505 by Lady Margaret Beaufort, mother of Henry VII, on the site of God's House. This devout woman founded the first professorship of divinity in the university, and her statue holding a bible, and coat of arms are on the gate. The shield is supported by mythical yales with goat's heads, antelope's bodies and elephants' tails. In the plasterwork are daisies (marguerites for Margaret) and forget-me-nots symbolising her motto *Souvent me Souvient*.

Enter **First Court**, built by 1511 but refaced in the 1750s. John Milton had rooms in the left-hand corner and Charles Darwin in the middle staircase on the right.

Go round the court to the **chapel** in the far left-hand corner. It is the original chapel of God's-house which was enlarged in 1506 and panelled in 1702. It has the original chestnut ceiling, and the glass in the north windows is some of the oldest in Cambridge. The east window (1912) shows the First Court with the Risen Christ above. The double memorial near the altar (1684) is to inseparable Fellows Sir John French and Sir Thomas Baines. Baines died in Constantinople, and French had his body embalmed and brought home so they could be buried together. The lectern is English – late fifteenth or early sixteenth century. A similar one is in St Mark's in Venice.

Leaving the chapel, walk straight ahead past the Master's Lodge on your left and turn left through the **dining-hall** screen. The hall was rebuilt in the last century, using some of the old panelling. It has portraits of former students Charles Darwin, Jan Smuts and John Milton, whose bust stands near the high table.

Continue into **Second Court**. The **Fellows' Building** (1642) is one of the earliest examples of classical architecture in Cambridge. The central gates lead to the **Fellows' Garden**, laid out in the early nineteenth century. It is generally open to visitors Monday to Friday 1030–1230 and 1400–1600. There are beehives, an old bathing-pool and in the far left-hand corner Milton's mulberry tree. It was probably planted when James I was trying to develop the silk industry. It is said that Milton, who came up to Christ's in 1628, sat under it while writing poetry.

Milton's mulberry tree, Christ's College

Retrace your steps and cross the road to walk along **Petty Cury**, which means 'Little Cookery'. In medieval times this was an extension of Cooks' Row on Market Hill. Pastry cooks had their stalls here. It was a busy road with shops and coaching-inns and was the first street in Cambridge to be paved with rounded cobbles in 1788. The Victorians demolished a number of inns, and in 1970 developers rebuilt the left-hand side of the old street as **The Lion Yard**, named after one of the demolished inns. The Red Lion himself standing in the centre of the precinct was a wooden template used for the lions at Waterloo Station in London.

Walk into **Market Hill**, the medieval centre of Cambridge. Here was the old guildhall and the prison with stocks and pillory outside. There was never any shortage of rotten fruit and vegetables to be thrown at those being punished.

Cambridge market is excellent. It is open every day and has a huge variety of stalls. On the front of the present

Guildhall (1937) are the arms of the City of Cambridge with the river and the all-important bridge. Walk round the Guildhall and return to the **Tourist Information Centre**.   □

Cambridge market-place

Walk 3

This is the suggested walking-tour for those times when some of the colleges are closed to visitors. You may find that King's College Chapel is open even though other college buildings are not. You will go to the Mill Pool, walk past some of the main college entrances, pausing at the Great Bridge near Magdalene College before returning to the city centre through fine shopping streets. Allow 2 to 2½ hours.

Turn right outside the **Tourist Information Centre**. Look right along **Peas Hill**, the medieval fish market and nothing like a 'hill'. Medieval Cambridge was low-lying, and this was above the marshy ground. 'Peas' is thought to come from *piscaria*, Latin for 'fish market'. There are enormous cellars under the road that were used as air-raid shelters during the Second World War. The Cambridge University Footlights stage their annual revue at the **Arts Theatre**.

Left into **Bene't** (short for Benedict) **Street**. At the medieval **Friars' House** look left up **Free School Lane**. There is the old **Cavendish Laboratory** (1847), one of the most famous laboratories in the world. In 1932 Ernest Rutherford led the team which split the atom for the first time, and in the 1950s Francis Crick and James Watson discovered the structure of DNA here. Turn round. Under roof guttering of No. 5 are three iron rings. If medieval timber buildings caught fire, hooks put in the rings were used to pull off the thatched roof to prevent the fire spreading.

The tower of **St Bene't's Church** on the left, with its Saxon long and short corner-stones, is the oldest building in the county, about 1025. The round holes above the double-belfry windows were used by nesting owls, which devoured the church mice! The churchyard is at medieval ground level. Streets were artificially raised above the floodline. Inside the church on your right is one of the old fire-hooks and a seventeenth-century coffin-stool. Fabian Stedman, parish clerk in 1670, invented change-ringing. The first organised peal of bells was probably rung from here. In the case in the right-hand corner is Thomas Hobson's Bible. He owned a livery stable and insisted his customers hired the horse nearest the door because that had rested longest. Hence the expression 'Hobson's choice' — no choice.

Cross the road under the carriage-arch into the courtyard of **The Eagle**, a former coaching-inn. Call in for a drink later and look at the ceiling in the Air Force Bar, where US and Allied airmen burned their names, squadron names and numbers with candles and cigarette-lighters during the Second World War. At the end of Bene't Street turn left.

On your left, **Corpus Christi College** (1352). Through the gate you get a glimpse of the **New Court**. The **chapel** door immediately opposite has statues either side. On the right is Matthew Parker, college Master in 1544 and Archbishop of Canterbury in the reign of Elizabeth I. A brilliant man who was always asking questions — from him we get the expression 'Nosey Parker'.

Next is **St Botolph's Church** (1320). Botolph was a seventh-century Saxon saint who became the patron saint of travellers. His churches were traditionally built beside city gates, where you prayed for a good

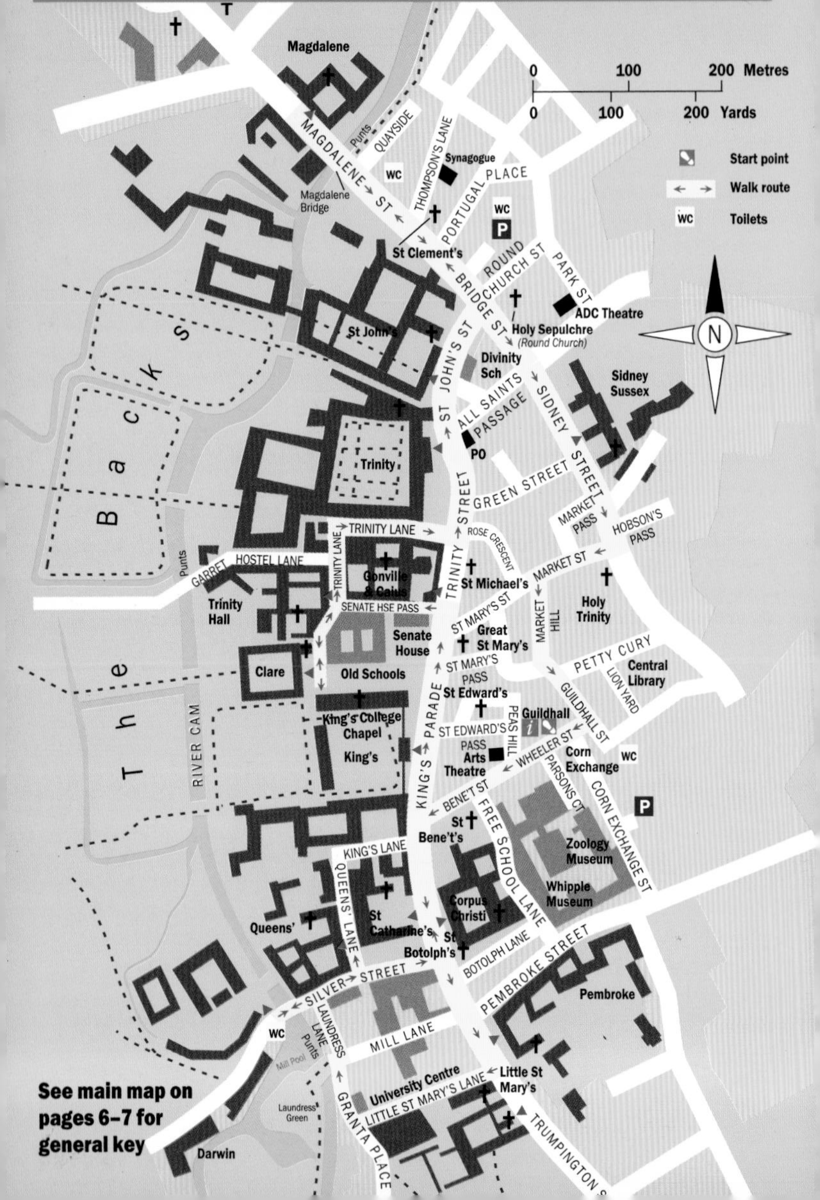

Magdalene

MAGDALENE ST

Punts
QUAYSIDE

THOMPSON'S LANE

WC

Synagogue

PORTUGAL PLACE

Magdalene
Bridge

WC

P

St Clement's

BRIDGE ST

ROUND CHURCH ST

PARK ST

St John's

ADC Theatre

Holy Sepulchre
(Round Church)

Divinity
Sch

ST JOHN'S ST

Sidney
Sussex

ALL SAINTS PASSAGE

SIDNEY STREET

PO

B
a
c
k
s

Trinity

GREEN STREET

MARKET PASS

HOBSON'S PASS

TRINITY LANE

Rose Crescent

TRINITY STREET

St Michael's

MARKET ST

Holy
Trinity

GARRET HOSTEL LANE

HOSTEL LANE

Gonville
& Caius

MARKET HILL

Trinity Hall

SENATE HSE PASS

Senate
House

St Mary's St

PETTY CURY

LION YARD

Central
Library

Great
St Mary's

Punts

Clare

Old Schools

ST MARY'S PASS

St Edward's

GUILDHALL ST

WC

P

CORN EXCHANGE ST

T
h
e

RIVER CAM

KING'S PARADE

King's College
Chapel

King's

ST EDWARD'S PASS

Guildhall

PEAS HILL

WHEELER ST

PARSONS CT

Corn
Exchange

BENET ST

Arts
Theatre

St
Benet's

FREE SCHOOL LANE

Zoology
Museum

KING'S LANE

Whipple
Museum

QUEENS' LANE

Queens'

St
Catharine's

Corpus
Christi

St
Botolph's

BOTOLPH LANE

PEMBROKE STREET

Pembroke

WC

SILVER STREET

LAUNDRESS LANE

Punts

MILL LANE

Mill Pool

Laundress
Green

University Centre

LITTLE ST MARY'S LANE

Little St
Mary's

TRUMPINGTON S

**See main map on
pages 6–7 for
general key**

Darwin

| 0 | | 100 | | 200 | Metres |

| 0 | | 100 | | 200 | Yards |

⬈ Start point

⟵ ⟶ Walk route

WC Toilets

N

journey and gave thanks for a safe return. Walk on and look back at the church roof with its old and unusual 'fish scale' tiles. On the tower are the evangelical emblems: the bull, the man, the eagle and the lion.

Botolph's Lane on your left has charming seventeenth-century houses and shops. No. 7 has a mysterious cut-out of a hanging man above the door. Why? Nobody seems to know.

Across the road on your right is the **Pitt Building**, part of the Cambridge University Press. Cambridge became the first university to have its own printing-press when Henry VIII gave it a royal warrant in 1534. The building is named after William Pitt the Younger, who came up to Pembroke College aged fourteen, was Chancellor of the Exchequer aged twenty-two and at twenty-four became our youngest Prime Minister. Continue along **Trumpington Street** and peep into Fitzbillies, long famous for their delicious Chelsea buns. Notice the channels either side of Trumpington Street, part of a seventeenth-century plan to bring fresh water into the centre of the city. Thomas Hobson gave money for this project.

On your left, **Pembroke College** (1347), founded by Marie de St Pol de Valence, the widowed Countess of Pembroke. At seventeen she married the fifty-year-old Earl. Legend says she was 'maid, wife and widow' all in one day, her husband being killed in front of her while jousting on their wedding-day.

The building at the end of the gatehouse range with the large window is the **chapel** — the first completed building by Christopher Wren. His uncle Mathew, Bishop of Ely, was imprisoned in the Tower of London for eighteen years by Oliver Cromwell. He

Fitzbillies

vowed that if he was released safely he would build a chapel in his old college. Naturally he asked his nephew to design it.

Cross Trumpington Street into **Little St Mary's Churchyard**. Cross the lawn on your left. Look up at the left-hand window of the top floor ahead of you, part of Peterhouse. Outside is a metal bar placed there for a fire escape by the poet Thomas Gray ('Elegy Written in a Country Churchyard') in 1756. When unsympathetic students pretended there was a fire, Gray was so upset he left Peterhouse and moved to Pembroke.

The first church on this site, St Peter-without-Trumpington-Gate was used by the next-door college, which took the name **Peterhouse**. In the fourteenth century the church was rebuilt and renamed the **Church of St Mary the Less** or Little St Mary's as it is affectionately called. Inside the church on your left is a memorial to Godfrey Washington, 'Minister of this Church and Fellow of St Peter's College', great-uncle of George Washington. Notice the family coat of arms, said to have inspired the flag of the United States — the Stars and Stripes. The churchyard is maintained as a wild garden by the residents of **Little St Mary's Lane**.

Go down the lane to the river. Notice the inn sign of the old Half Moon pub, the original gas street lights which burn constantly and the attractive sixteenth-, seventeenth- and eighteenth-century cottages. At the bottom on your left is the prestigious **Garden House Moat House Hotel**. Turn right past the modern **Cambridge University Centre** (1967). Across the **River Cam** on **Laundress Green** the laundry-women once spread their washing out to dry. The Old Granary opposite was the home of Charles Darwin's eldest son. Since 1964 it has been part of **Darwin College**, the first graduate college in the university.

For centuries the **Mill Pool** here was the scene of frantic commercial activity. Today this part of the river is reserved for punts, rowing-boats and canoes. You can pole your own hired punt or have a 'chauffeur'.

Up **Laundress Lane**. The small, high window in the brick tower ahead is known as Erasmus's window. He was here in 1510 and complained that the wine tasted like vinegar, beer was even worse, his expenses were enormous and his profits not a brass farthing. But he did think the Cambridge women were nice to kiss!

Turn left into **Silver Street**, cross the road to see the **Mathematical Bridge** (1749) in **Queens' College**. The story is that the original bridge had no nails to hold it together, the students took it down and the college could not put it together again so they used bolts. Sadly this is untrue. The present bridge of 1905 was built to the original design which had bolts at the main joints.

Go back up Silver Street, turning left into **Queens' Lane** to the Gate Tower of Queens' College. Queens' was refounded by two

Mill Pool

King's College gate and stone screen

queens, Margaret of Anjou, wife of Henry VI, in 1448 and Elizabeth of Woodville, wife of Edward IV, in 1465 hence the plural spelling of 'Queens' College'. But the original founder, Andrew Dokett, has his likeness carved over the entrance gate.

Return to Silver Street and continue up it. Across the road is the university **Department of Applied Mathematics and Theoretical Physics**. Ede & Ravenscroft on the corner have been making academic robes since 1689. They hold the four royal warrants of the British royal family and have made the coronation robes of every sovereign since William III.

Left into **King's Parade** past the wrought-iron railings of **St Catharine's College** (1473) on your left, with her golden Catharine wheel above the gate. William Wotton of St Catharine's was the youngest

undergraduate ever to come to Cambridge University. Born in 1666, he knew Latin, Greek and Hebrew at the age of six and came to Cambridge aged nine. The modern buildings on your left are partly on the site of Thomas Hobson's stable. Look at the splendidly varied range of buildings along King's Parade on your right and on the left the nineteenth-century stone screen and gatehouse of **King's College** (1441). Right of the gateway is a nineteenth-century hexagonal post-box with 'VR' - *Victoria Regina*. Even though the college is closed, the **chapel**, whose majestic east end with its twin pinnacles rises on your left, may be open. We visit it later on this walk.

The last shop on the right is Ryder & Amies, university outfitters. In its windows are the university sporting fixture lists showing which students have been chosen for the various university teams.

Great St Mary's, the University Church, is late Gothic Perpendicular built between 1478 and 1519. The tower, finished later, is often open to the public. Climb the 123 steps to the top for spectacular views of the city and colleges. The quarter chimes on the 1793 clock were subsequently copied for Big Ben at Westminster and are now called 'Westminster chimes' but Cambridge had them first! The circle cut to the right of the west door in the outside tower wall is a datum point. This is the centre of Cambridge from which all distances are measured.

Until 1730, degrees were awarded in Great St Mary's, and the University Sermons are still preached here each term. Inside the church the roof is made of timbers given by Henry VII. As the number of students increased, more seating was needed. The galleries, added in 1735, have special seats so the university proctors, responsible for discipline, could watch the students during services. The pulpit runs on rails to the middle of the church so the preacher of the University Sermon can be seen from both galleries. Protestant reformers Thomas Cranmer, Hugh Latimer and Nicholas Ridley all preached in Great St Mary's. They were Cambridge men all burned for heresy in Oxford in the reign of Mary Tudor. Near the altar a plaque shows where German Protestant reformer Martin Bucer (or Butzer) was buried. Mary Tudor had him exhumed, his coffin was tied to a stake in the market-place and burned. In the reign of Elizabeth I soil from the market square was put in a coffin and Bucer was 'reburied' in the church. The original windows were destroyed by the Puritans, the present ones are nineteenth century. Behind the altar is

the Majestas, a modern gilded wooden carving showing the risen Christ standing before a cross which has sprouted leaves to symbolise the Tree of Life.

Return to King's Parade. The corner bookshop beyond the church now belongs to the Cambridge University Press. This is the site of the oldest bookshop in Britain. Books have been sold here since 1581.

Across the road from Great St Mary's is the heart of Cambridge University. Facing you is the **Old Schools**, standing on the first land bought by the university. Behind the eighteenth-century classical façade are the oldest university buildings in Cambridge built in the late fourteenth century. End on to the road is the elegant **Senate House** (1730) designed by James Gibbs. Here the Council of the Senate, the governing body of the university, meets. Students wearing their gowns come here to be awarded their degrees, and honorary degrees are given here annually. Examination results are posted on wooden boards beneath the Senate House windows. In 1958 engineering students hoisted a small car onto the roof of the Senate House overnight. It took the astonished authorities a week to get it down.

Turn left into **Senate House Passage**. The splendid gate on the right is the Gate of Honour of **Gonville and Caius College**. Dr Caius (pronounced 'Keys') refounded the college in 1557 with three gates symbolising a student's academic life. He entered through the Gate of Humility, passed under the Gate of Virtue and finally through the Gate of Honour to receive his degree. Turn and look back up Senate House Passage. The gap between the small, dark turret of Gonville and Caius on the left and the far end of the Senate

Trinity College's Great Court

House roof on the right is the Senate House Leap, traditionally jumped by night-climbing students. Night climbing has long been an illegal pastime in Cambridge.

At the bottom of the Passage, bear left. The large gateway on your left, which now leads to the university's administrative offices, was the original gatehouse of King's College Old Court. Ahead is the entrance to **King's College** and **Chapel**. If you wish to enter the college, please turn to p. 94. To continue the walk after your visit leave King's by this gate.

On the left, **Clare College** (1326), the second oldest Cambridge college, refounded twelve years later by Lady Elizabeth de Clare. Her lozenge on the gate is encircled by a black mourning-band with gold tear-drops. Poor Lady Elizabeth was always crying — she had three husbands, and they all died before she was thirty.

Continue walking and the next college on the left is **Trinity Hall**, founded in 1350 to help counter the ravages of the Black Death among lawyers and churchmen. Trinity Hall is known as the lawyers' college.

Walk on and turn right up **Trinity Lane**. The gate on your left is sometimes open, giving a splendid view of **Trinity College Great Court**, covering over 2 acres *0.8 ha*. Across the court is King Edward III's Gate. He is holding a sword with three crowns to show he considered himself king of England, France and Scotland. The large clock above him has a double strike, low note then high; William Wordsworth calls it the clock with a 'male and female voice'. While it is striking 12 o'clock (i.e. twenty-four times), students try to run round the Great Court — 380 yards *347.5 m* in 43 seconds. Only the late Marquis of Exeter has succeeded. The run was featured in the film *Chariots of Fire*, but Harold Abrahams never attempted it, and the sequence was not filmed here. The college **chapel** to the right of King Edward's Gate

Laura Ashley's

was built by Mary Tudor and her sister Elizabeth. As a student here Lord Byron reputedly swam in the central fountain. Undergraduates were not permitted to keep dogs in college (they still are not) so Byron bought a bear and kept it in a college attic. The steps on the left lead to the college **dining-hall** (1604). The roof lantern allowed smoke from the brazier in the hall to escape.

Continue up Trinity Lane and turn left. Hobbs sports shop on the corner was started by Sidney, brother of the famous cricketer Sir Jack Hobbs. On the right, Laura Ashley's was once an inn called the Turk's Head, where wealthy aristocratic undergraduate members of 'The True Blue and Beefsteak Club' ate gargantuan dinners washed down with gallons of wine. The Blue Boar on the right was a coaching-inn and Heffers Children's Bookshop on the left has a superb late eighteenth-century shop-front. Turn left onto the cobbles

outside the Great Gate of **Trinity College**, founded in 1546 by Henry VIII as one of the last acts of his life — he died six weeks later. Look at his statue on the gate. What is he holding in his right hand? A chair-leg put there by students long ago when they exchanged it for his sceptre. The shields and coats of arms are those of Edward III – who founded an earlier college on the site – and his six sons. The blank shield was for William of Hatfield who died in infancy. Look right. The small tree in the middle of the lawn, planted in the 1950s, is a descendant of the apple-tree under which Isaac Newton was sitting at his home in Woolsthorpe, Lincolnshire, when, according to tradition, an apple hitting him on the head led him to discover the laws of gravity.

Newton came to Trinity in 1661. His rooms were to the right of the Great Gate. Trinity College has produced thirty-one Nobel prize-winners but it is generally accepted that Newton was the greatest of all Cambridge scholars. HRH The Prince of Wales is a Trinity man.

The next gate-tower is **St John's** (1511). Above the gate, St John's statue has his emblem, the eagle, at his feet. The coat of arms of the foundress, Lady Margaret Beaufort, is supported by mythical yales, with goats' heads, antelopes' bodies and elephants' tails. Their horns move independently. There are daisies (marguerites) and forget-me-nots, symbolising her motto *Souvent me Souvient*. Can you spot a fox entering its lair above the nose of the yale on the right?

Continue turning left down **Bridge Street** towards the river. On your left is **St John's College Chapel** (1869). At noon on Ascension Day the college choir sings hymns from the top of the tower.

St John's College gate

Underneath the road are timbers laid by the Romans to cross marshy land. They are often uncovered during roadworks.

Stand on the **Great Bridge** over the river Cam. The first bridge here was a wooden one built in the middle of the 800s. In 1754 there was a stone bridge, and the present bridge built in 1823 needs strengthening periodically to carry heavy traffic. This is the place where the city got its name: River 'Cam' plus 'bridge' – 'Cambridge'.

On your left upriver are some of the modern buildings of St John's College. Downriver on your right is **The Quayside**. For centuries a busy area when Cambridge was a seaport, it is now redeveloped into riverside flats, shops and restaurants. You can hire punts here.

Opposite The Quayside is **Magdalene College** (1542). It was the last all-male college. When they admitted women in 1988 the men wore black armbands at the beginning of term and flew the college flag at half mast. Magdalene was Samuel Pepys' old college. He left them his library of 3,000 books, including his famous diary.

Return up **Bridge Street**, passing **St Clement's Church**, first mentioned in 1218. St Clement is the patron saint of Danish seafarers, and the church stands on the site of the early Viking settlement. Look at the range of beautifully restored medieval buildings on your left.

Magdalene College

On the corner is the **Church of the Holy Sepulchre**, one of four surviving 'round' churches in England. The round nave and aisle were built in the first half of the twelfth century. Eight massive Norman pillars have slender double Norman arches above them. The east window of 1946 shows Christ crucified on a living tree — the Tree of Life — and replaces a Victorian window blown out by a wartime bomb. The church was extensively restored in the 1840s.

Leaving the church, turn left. A footpath leads to the famous **Union Society**, where many leading politicians began their careers in the debating-chamber. Continue into **Sidney Street**. On your left is **Sidney Sussex College** (1596). Oliver Cromwell was an undergraduate here, and in 1960 his head was buried secretly in the ante-chapel.

Continue along Sidney Street. In the nineteenth century the street was full of elegant houses and shops. The 1920s saw huge demolition, and many old businesses disappeared. Look left down **Sussex Street**.

The modern high-level covered bridge links two parts of Sidney Sussex College.

Turn right into **Market Street**, one of the city's oldest shopping streets, called Shoemakers' Lane in 1592. **Holy Trinity Church** is on your left. The original twelfth-century building was destroyed in the great fire of 1174. Charles Simeon of the evangelical movement was minister here from 1782 to 1836. He was one of the first people to use an umbrella. That and his teapot are in the vestry.

Continue into the **Market Hill**. The medieval guildhall stood here and the prison with its stocks and pillory — there was always plenty of rotten fruit and vegetables to throw at criminals. The excellent market is open every day and sells a remarkable variety of goods.

On the front of the present **Guildhall** (1937) is the city's coat of arms with the river and all-important bridge on it. Behind the Guildhall is the **Tourist Information Centre**, and you are back where you started.   □

Sidney Sussex College

Walk 4

This walk is designed to show the visitor the beauties of the Backs if the colleges are closed. Please remember that King's College Chapel is often open when other buildings are closed. This walk will take you to the chapel should you wish to visit it. Allow 2 to 2½ hours.

Turn right outside the **Tourist Information Centre**. Look right along **Peas Hill**, the medieval fish market and nothing like a 'hill'. Medieval Cambridge was low-lying, and this was above the marshy ground. 'Peas' is thought to come from *piscaria*, Latin for 'fish market'. There are enormous cellars under the road that were used as air-raid shelters during the Second World War. The Cambridge University Footlights stage their annual revue at the **Arts Theatre**, and this important little provincial theatre presents a varied programme of drama, opera and music throughout the year.

Left into **Bene't** (short for Benedict) **Street**. At the medieval **Friars' House** look left up **Free School Lane**. There is the old **Cavendish Laboratory** (1847), one of the most famous laboratories in the world. In 1932 Ernest Rutherford led the team which split the atom for the first time, and in the 1950s Francis Crick and James Watson discovered the structure of DNA here. Turn round. Under roof guttering of No. 5 are three iron rings. If medieval timber buildings caught fire, hooks put in the rings were used to pull off the thatched roof to prevent the fire spreading.

The tower of **St Bene't's Church** on the left, with its Saxon long and short corner-stones, is the oldest building in the county,

Tourist Information Centre

about 1025. The round holes above the double-belfry windows were once used by nesting owls, which devoured the church mice! The churchyard is at medieval ground level. Streets were artificially raised above the floodline. Inside the church on your right is one of the old fire-hooks and a seventeenth-century coffin-stool. Fabian Stedman, parish clerk in 1670, invented change-ringing. The first organised peal of bells was probably rung from here. In the case in the right-hand corner is Thomas Hobson's Bible. He owned a livery stable and insisted his customers hired the horse nearest the door because that had rested longest. Hence the expression 'Hobson's choice' — no choice.

Cross the road under the carriage-arch into the courtyard of **The Eagle**, a former coaching-inn. Call in for a drink later and look at the ceiling in the Air Force Bar, where US and Allied airmen burned their names, squadron names and numbers with candles and cigarette-lighters during the Second World War.

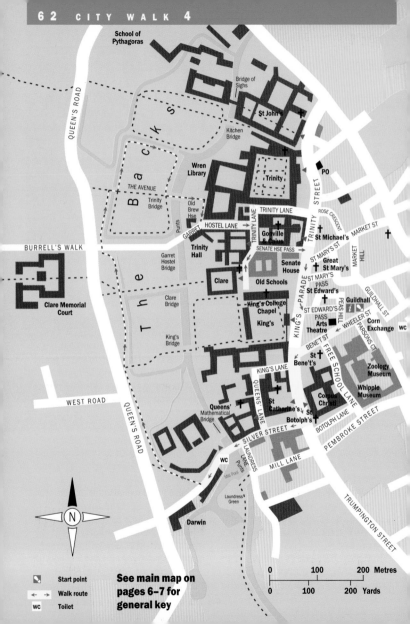

School of Pythagoras

Bridge of Sighs

St John's

Kitchen Bridge

Wren Library

Trinity

B a c k s

THE AVENUE

Trinity Bridge

Old Brew Hse

TRINITY LANE

HOSTEL LANE

Gonville & Caius

St Michael's

PO

TRINITY STREET

ROSE CRESCENT

MARKET ST

BURRELL'S WALK

GARRET HOSTEL LANE

Trinity Hall

Garret Hostel Bridge

SENATE HSE PASS

Senate House

St Mary's Pass

Great St Mary's

MARKET HILL

T h e   B a c k s

Clare

Clare Bridge

Old Schools

ST MARY'S PASS

St Edward's

GUILDHALL ST

King's College Chapel

King's

ST EDWARD'S PASS

Guildhall
i

Corn Exchange

WC

PEAS HILL

WHEELER ST

PARSONS CT

King's Bridge

KING'S PARADE

Arts Theatre

Zoology Museum

BENET'S ST

WEST ROAD

KING'S LANE

St Bene't's

FREE SCHOOL LANE

Clare Memorial Court

QUEEN'S ROAD

Queens' Mathematical Bridge

QUEENS' LANE

St Catharine's

Corpus Christi

Whipple Museum

St Botolph's

BOTOLPH LANE

PEMBROKE STREET

SILVER STREET

WC

LAUNDRESS LANE

Punts

Mill Pond

MILL LANE

TRUMPINGTON STREET

Laundress Green

Darwin

N

| | Start point |
| WC | Toilet |
→ ← Walk route

See main map on pages 6–7 for general key

| 0 | 100 | 200 Metres |
| 0 | 100 | 200 Yards |

St Catharine's College

At the end of Bene't Street, turn left. The modern buildings across the road on the right are on the site of Hobson's stables. The college on the right is **St Catharine's** (1473) with her gilded Catharine wheel in the wrought-iron gate. William Wotton of St Catharine's was the youngest undergraduate ever to come to Cambridge University. Born 1666, he knew Latin, Greek and Hebrew at the age of six and came to Cambridge aged nine.

On your left, **Corpus Christi College** (1352). Through the gate you get a glimpse of the **New Court**. The chapel door immediately opposite has statues either side. On the right is Matthew Parker, college Master in 1544 and Archbishop of Canterbury in the reign of Elizabeth I. A brilliant man who was always asking questions — from him we get the expression 'Nosey Parker'.

Next is **St Botolph's Church** (1320). Botolph was a seventh-century Saxon saint who became the patron saint of travellers. His churches were traditionally built beside city gates, where you prayed for a good journey and gave thanks for a safe return.

Cross the road to Ede & Ravenscroft, who have been making academic robes since 1689. They hold the four royal warrants of the British royal family and have made the coronation robes of every sovereign since William III.

Look across the road to the church-like **Pitt Building** (named after William Pitt the Younger), part of the Cambridge University Press. Cambridge became the first university to have its own printing-press when Henry VIII gave them a royal warrant in 1534. Students sometimes call this building 'the freshers' church'. New students are told that if they want to hear the best sermon in Cambridge on the first Sunday of term this is the church to come to!

Walk down **Silver Street**. On your left, the university **Department of Applied Mathematics and Theoretical Physics**. Turn right into **Queens' Lane**. Queens'

College was refounded by two queens, Margaret of Anjou, wife of Henry VI, in 1448 and Elizabeth of Woodville, wife of Edward IV, in 1465 hence the plural spelling of 'Queens' College'. But the original founder, Andrew Dokett, has his likeness carved over the entrance gate on this gatehouse of 1448.

Return to Silver Street and walk to the bridge. On your right is the famous wooden **Mathematical Bridge** of Queens' College. The story was that the original bridge had no nails to hold it together, the students took it down and the college could not put it together again so they used bolts. Sadly this is untrue. The present bridge of 1905 was built to the original design of 1749 which had bolts at the main joints.

Left of the bridge is the modern **Cripps Court**, built in the 1970s. Cross Silver Street – carefully – to look down at the **Mill Pool**. For centuries the Mill Pool was a scene of frantic commercial activity. Today this part of the river is reserved for punts, rowing-boats and canoes. You can pole your own hired punt or have a 'chauffeur'.

The grass beyond the pond is **Laundress Green**, where the laundry-women once spread their washing out to dry. The present Silver Street bridge was built in 1932 but there have been bridges here since the fourteenth century. On the annual Rag Day the students wear fancy dress and collect money for charity. They have a competition to see who can 'fly' the furthest from the bridge before dropping into the water.

Mathematical Bridge, Queens' College

The first building on your right is a new library for **Darwin College** built with old bricks (1994). The next is the **Old Granary**, home of Charles Darwin's eldest son. Since 1964 it has been part of Darwin College, the first graduate college in the university.

Turn round and cross over Silver Street on the pedestrian crossing. Turn left and follow the path until it veers right onto **Queens' Green** and on past the modern development on your right which houses squash courts and a conference centre.

On your right across the narrow stream

Scholars' Piece,
King's College

is **Queens' Grove**, part of the world-famous **Backs** of Cambridge, called that for the simple reason that they are the backs of six of the riverside colleges. They used to be called the Backsides. In spring, the Backs are a mass of early flowers — aconites, snowdrops, grape hyacinths, crocuses, daffodils and tulips — and each season is beautiful in its own special way.

Continue along the path until you have passed the wrought-iron gate of **King's College** and here, before you, is the most famous view in the whole of Cambridge — **King's College and King's College Chapel with Clare College** – 'more palace than college' – on the left, completing the picture. **Scholars' Piece**, the meadow in front of you, belongs to King's College. In summer, sheep and cattle graze peacefully as visitors stand and stare. The land on which King's College stands was the medieval city centre with houses, shops, narrow, crowded streets, a church and wharves along the river. All this was cleared when Henry VI decided it was the ideal site for his new college in 1441. In 1446 Henry laid the foundation-stone of his new chapel, which took almost 100 years to complete.

The chapel is Perpendicular Gothic. The classical **Gibbs' Fellows' Building** on the right, designed in 1724, is a perfect foil for the chapel and provides a startling contrast in architectural styles.

Continue along the path. The relatively young trees on the grass on your left replaced mature elms cut down when they were ravaged by Dutch elm disease.

The next college is **Clare** (1326), the second oldest college in Cambridge. The avenue of trees from the gate to the river was laid out in 1690. Clare's **Fellows' Garden**, sometimes open to the public, is a delight.

Across **Queen's Road** on the left is **Memorial Court** (1924) built in memory of the Clare men killed in the First World War. The tall tower beyond Memorial Court is the **University Library**. It was built in the 1930s when the original library became too small. It has been a 'copyright' library since 1709 and is entitled to receive free of charge a copy of every book published in the country. Its constantly growing collection requires almost 2 miles *3.2 km* of new shelf-space every year.

Continue along the path, crossing **Garret Hostel Lane**, to the next wrought-iron gate. Go through it onto **Trinity College Backs**. The 1672 avenue of lime-trees was replanted in 1949. (If for any reason Trinity College should be closed to visitors, retrace your steps and turn left into Garret Hostel Lane, crossing the river to rejoin the walk.) **Trinity**, founded by Henry VIII in 1546, has more students than any other college and has produced thirty-one Nobel prize-winners. Isaac Newton, Cambridge's most famous student, was an undergraduate here. Follow the path round to your left for a view of Trinity Backs, laid out in the late seventeenth century and early eighteenth century, and the **Wren Library** across the river. Designed by Christopher Wren and completed in 1695, the library contains 55,000 books printed before 1820, 2,500 volumes of early manuscripts — and A.A. Milne's manuscript of *Winnie the Pooh*. Milne and his son Christopher Robin were both Trinity men. The library is generally open to visitors Monday to Friday 1200–1400, Saturdays in full term 1030–1230.

Walk along to the small iron bridge for a view of **St John's College Backs** and **New Court**, built in the 1820s in Gothic Revival style and promptly nicknamed 'The

Trinity College Bridge

Wedding Cake'. Walk back along the river-bank to **Trinity Bridge**. You will not see any racing eights on this part of the river — the college crews practise downstream.

Cross the bridge and leave Trinity College through the double wooden gates on the right into Garret Hostel Lane. Straight ahead is the re-erected fourteenth-century gateway of **Trinity Hall**. The main gates were kept open in normal times but closed when 'town and gown' trouble began. Then the smaller gates on the left were opened. However, if serious riots threatened, only the tiny wicket-door was opened — it is called 'the eye of the needle'.

Left up Garret Hostel Lane. This narrow Lane was given to the town by Henry VI as their only access to this part of the river after he demolished the centre of the city. It is a two-way street, used by carts in medieval times — you can see where they scraped the old walls — and lorries today — you can see their marks at the corner of Garret Hostel and Trinity lanes. Turn right into Trinity Lane, passing the front entrance

to Trinity Hall, founded in 1350 by the Bishop of Norwich.

If you have not been into King's College Chapel and would like to visit it, continue along Trinity Lane, passing on your left the original gatehouse of King's College and the main entrance to Clare College on your right (see p. 84). When you leave King's College, return here to continue the walk.

If you have already visited King's College, turn left and walk up **Senate House Passage**. Look ahead to the end of the passage. The gap between the small, dark turret of **Gonville and Caius College** on the left and the far end of the **Senate House** roof on your right is the 'Senate House Leap', traditionally jumped by night-climbing undergraduates.

The splendid gate on the left is the Gate of Honour of **Gonville and Caius College**. Dr Caius (pronounced 'Keys') refounded the college in 1557 with three gates symbolising a student's academic life. The student entered through the Gate of Humility, passed under the Gate of Virtue

Senate House Passage

and finally through the Gate of Honour to receive his degree.

Turn right. This is the heart of the University of Cambridge. The classical building on your right is the **Senate House** designed by James Gibbs (1730). Here the Council of the Senate, the governing body of the university, meets, students wearing their gowns come here to be awarded their degrees, and honorary degrees are given here annually. Examination results are posted on wooden boards beneath the Senate House windows. In 1958 engineering students hoisted a small car onto the Senate House roof overnight. It took the authorities nearly a whole week to get the car down.

Left of the Senate House facing the road is the **Old Schools**, standing on the first land bought by the university. Behind the eighteenth-century classical façade are the oldest university buildings in Cambridge, built in the late fourteenth century.

Turn round. The corner bookshop on the left now belongs to the Cambridge University Press. This is the site of the oldest bookshop in Britain. Books have been sold here since 1581.

Great St Mary's, the **University Church**, is late Gothic Perpendicular, built between 1478 and 1519. The 114-foot *35-m* high tower, finished later, is often open to the public. Climb the 123 steps to the top for spectacular views of the city and colleges. Until 1730, degrees were awarded here. The University Sermons are still preached here each term. A curfew bell was rung every night at 9 o'clock, after which all students had to be back in college. The quarter chimes on the 1793 clock were subsequently copied for Big Ben at Westminster and are now called 'Westminster chimes' — but Cambridge had them first!

Walk to the right along **King's Parade** with its splendidly varied range of buildings on the left and on the right the east end of **King's College Chapel** and the nineteenth-century stone screen and gatehouse of **King's College**. The first shop is Ryder & Amies,

Hexagonal post-box

university outfitters. In its windows are the university sporting fixture lists showing which students have been chosen for the various university teams. To the right of King's gatehouse is a nineteenth-century hexagonal post-box with 'VR' — *Victoria Regina*.

Turn left into **St Edward's Passage**. Clothiers on the corner is a university outfitter's. They supply the Cambridge University Boat Race crew and many university teams with their blazers, scarves and pullovers. (The word 'blazer' comes from St John's College, whose boat club have always worn scarlet jackets, i.e. blazers). On your right up St Edward's Passage is the quaint Haunted Bookshop. When you reach **St Edward's Church**, notice on your left the amusing lintel above the door into Mowbray's Bookshop.

The oldest part of the Church of St Edward King and Martyr is the thirteenth-century tower now cement rendered. The church was closely associated with the early reformers, and Hugh Latimer

David's bookshop

preached from the pulpit. Facing the church on the left of the square is the celebrated David's bookshop.

Turn right into **Peas Hill** and left to the **Tourist Information Centre**, where this tour ends. ☐

Riverside walks

The towpaths and commons beside the river provide opportunities for strolls and longer walks. From the Quayside at Magdalene Bridge it is possible to walk on the wooden walkway beside the river to Jesus Green. From there you can cross Midsummer and Stourbridge commons to a footpath which gives access to a towpath on the left bank. The river can be recrossed at Baitsbite Lock to return through Fen Ditton.

Closer to the town centre are various paths which cross the commons which

extend south from Silver Street Bridge.

At the end of Grantchester Street a field footpath leads to the village of Grantchester where Rupert Brooke lived in the Old Vicarage. Just through the village on the Grantchester–Trumpington Road, a footpath leads to Byron's Pool, the place where the poet is supposed to have swum when he was a student at Cambridge.

The Tourist Information Centre sells leaflets with maps describing these and other local walks.

The University of Cambridge and the colleges

Edward III's Gate, Trinity College

The University of Cambridge and the colleges are completely separate yet inextricably intertwined: a statement which, as we shall see, is not the enigmatic contradiction in terms which it appears to be.

But before we look for the explanation, it will be as well to examine a few examples of Cambridge terminology which will help the visitor to understand the university and collegiate systems more easily ...

Chancellor: the supreme head of the university, normally a person of high rank who usually makes an appearance only on ceremonial and other important occasions, although the present holder of the office, HRH Prince Philip, the Duke of Edinburgh, shows a deep and continuing interest in all aspects of university life and makes many private visits to Cambridge. Elected for life by the Senate.

Vice-Chancellor: the active head of the university, the 'managing director' in charge of the day-to-day running of 'the firm'. Elected from among the heads of the houses or colleges, the Vice-Chancellor now serves for a maximum period of seven years.

Heads of houses: house here means college. The majority of colleges term their heads Master but other names are Provost, President, Mistress, Principal and Warden. Most heads are elected by the Fellowship (Fellows) other than at Trinity and Churchill colleges, which are Crown appointments, and Magdalene whose Master is appointed by the College Visitor.

Chair: a professorship.

Don: loosely, a graduate who is a university or college teacher, a senior member.

Fellows: today a Fellow can be male or female. It is a college term and generally it will be a graduate or senior member holding teaching or administrative office within the college. Fellows share in the government of the college.

Terms: there are three official Cambridge terms: Michaelmas (Oct–Dec), Lent (Jan–March) and Easter (April–June).

Undergraduates: student members of the university who have not taken a degree — graduates, those who have.

Freshers: first-year undergraduates.

Esquire bedells: official and ceremonial processions involving the Chancellor or Vice-Chancellor are led by two esquire bedells carrying on their shoulders the splendid silver maces presented by a former chancellor, the Duke of Buckingham, in 1616. The now purely ceremonial office was first mentioned in 1250.

Proctors: another ancient office — holders of it are listed continuously from 1314. Responsible for centuries for maintaining good order and discipline, their powers are now somewhat diminished. They are supported in their duties by ...

'Bulldogs': really university constables, they were once chosen for their athletic qualities for they were often required to chase erring undergraduates. You will recognise them on ceremonial occasions for they carry the senior and junior proctors' insignia which include heavily bound volumes of the 1785 edition of the university statutes.

'The Other Place': the Cambridge name for Oxford. After nearly 800 years of amicable rivalry many Cambridge folk still refuse to allow the other great and ancient university the dignity of a name!

Courts: to be found inside the colleges, courts are spaces enclosed by walls or buildings. In the other place the name would be a quad or quadrangle.

Combination room: peculiar to Cambridge, the term describes a room, normally close by the dining-hall, where Fellows and their guests may 'combine' together after meals, take perhaps a glass of port or other wine and converse. In St John's College, the Senior Combination Room is 93 feet *28.3 m* long and lit only by candles.

High table: students normally eat at tables positioned lengthways down the dining-hall while the head of the college and other senior members and guests eat at a table across one end of the room. Traditionally the high table is raised a few inches above those of the students so that the younger members of the college can look up to their betters.

May balls, May races: being Cambridge. the May balls and May rowing races are always held in June after the examinations when there are great festivities. May balls are held inside the colleges where there is dancing all night, splendid food, champagne and other entertainments. Since a third of all undergraduates leave Cambridge each year at the end of their three-year degree course May Week in June provides the final memories of their student days — and nights.

Punts: flat-bottomed boats propelled by pushing a long pole into the river-bed. No visit to Cambridge is complete without a punt trip. Self-propelled and 'chauffeured' punts are available.

Porters: college gatekeepers and guardians of good behaviour – especially among tourists! – inside the colleges. They are recognisable in some colleges by their traditional bowler hats.

Tripos: another name peculiar to

May Ball

Cambridge, a tripos is a university examination which, if passed, leads to the honours Bachelor of Arts degree. Until the late eighteenth century, examinations were oral and a candidate had to 'dispute' a proposition with an older graduate who always sat on a three-legged stool. The Greco-Latin name for the stool — *tripos*. Today's written exams still bear the name, i.e. the English Tripos, the Mathematical Tripos, etc.

Bedders: or bedmakers, the name for generations of women who have worked part-time performing domestic chores in the colleges. Because of the danger of temptation when all the students were male, the university issued an edict in 1635 forbidding

Porter

women under 50 to 'make any bed or perform any other service within any scholar's chamber'. The long-believed story that the university insisted all bedmakers should be 'old, married and ugly' is perhaps a malicious calumny. Although everybody likes to believe the tale, it is most certainly not true of today's bedders.

University and colleges – the relationship

So, back to the initial conundrum. Let us seek an answer.

The university is a self-governing body funded mainly by the state and granted its power to award degrees by the Crown. Its statutes can only be changed with the agreement of the Queen in Council. (Oddly, the Queen is the only person who cannot be awarded an honorary degree by the university since she is the fount of all honours.) Only the university may set examinations. The greater part of the teaching of undergraduates is now the prerogative of the university, but what the university cannot do is admit students to Cambridge. That is the prerogative of the colleges.

Any student wishing to attend the university must apply for admission to a college. Once admitted to a college the student is then a member of the university. Thus we have the paradox of a university responsible for the bulk of the teaching of its members but which is not allowed to admit them.

Many visitors ask to be shown 'the university' but there is no university campus in Cambridge. The different faculties and departments with their lecture rooms, laboratories and libraries have evolved over 800 years and are spread all over the city. This is why today Cambridge has one of the most concentrated bicycle populations in Europe with students dashing out from their colleges after breakfast and heading in every direction for tuition.

The teaching staff of the university – professors, readers, lecturers, assistant lecturers and demonstrators together with administrative, technical and clerical staff – are employees of the university. But many of them are also members of colleges where they hold teaching appointments, the remuneration for which is provided by the college.

The colleges are private, corporate bodies owning their own buildings and generating their own incomes. Fiercely independent and self-governing, they are regulated by their own statutes – but these statutes can only be changed after consultation with the university and with the approval of the Queen in Council.

Today. the colleges are primarily 'homes' for their students, providing lodgings, a dining-hall, a library and, generally, a chapel. Every aspect of student welfare is catered for by the college. Within its walls is to be found the whole fascinating fabric of student life: theatre, music, sport, debating societies, political clubs, dining clubs and so on. Further, because students study or 'read' their subjects mainly within the university, the college becomes a community in which young people can meet, live and harmonise outside the strict confines of intellectual subjects. This is why Cambridge students quickly find they owe their allegiance firstly to their college and secondly to the university.

College teaching

There is, however, a further and enormously important facet of college life, namely the individual and small-group tuition which is given within the college. In addition to university teaching each student receives 'supervisions' within his or her college. Attendance at lectures in arts subjects in the university is optional but students are expected to attend supervisions in college and to produce written work for their supervisors throughout their degree course.

Thus we have the two separate bodies, university and the colleges, linked by the student body and by teaching staff who are, in the main, members of both institutions. There are other links. At the student level there are many university societies, there is university theatre and music and, of course, sport. All colleges have their own sports facilities but sportsmen and women who excel will be chosen to play for the university. Those who represent the university against Oxford are awarded a 'blue', though some minor sports merit only a half blue. The two annual sporting encounters between Oxford and Cambridge which attract national attention are the rugby match at Twickenham and the Boat Race on the River Thames.

At the senior level we have seen that many dons are members of both institutions, and the link is strengthened through their membership of the university's many boards and committees.

Although the student population is likely to rise slightly in the future, at present it consists of about 11,500 undergraduates (6,150 men and 5,350 women) and 4,820 graduates (2,750 men and 2,070 women), with one-tenth of the total coming from more than 100 different countries outside the United Kingdom.

Senate House

Student costs at Cambridge are similar to those of other UK universities, and arrangements for financial support of UK and EU students are the same for Cambridge students as they are at other UK universities. Cambridge costings have three elements: university fees, college fees and maintenance expenses. The total average annual cost of the three elements in 2000 for UK and EU students at Cambridge was £5,630. For overseas students from outside the EU minimum annual resources required were between £15,000 and £20,000, depending upon the subject being studied. There is a national scheme for support of UK students in higher education, which applies partially to students from other member states of the EU. Some colleges offer partial support for overseas students.

How the colleges work

Colleges derive their incomes from past benefactions, from investments and from fees paid by students, and are governed by a Master (or Mistress, Provost, President or Warden) and a number of Fellows. A Praelector is considered to be the 'father' of the college, and it is this officer who leads undergraduates into the Senate House to receive their degrees. The bursar is responsible for financial affairs, investments, buildings and land. There is often a junior bursar to share the work-load. Tutors are not what they sound — they are not teachers, rather they are 'guardians', there to look after a group of students and oversee their general welfare. They act in the role of a parent during the student's college career — in loco parentis — although that term is considered old-fashioned now that adulthood arrives earlier with undergraduates. Every undergraduate is assigned to a Director of Studies who is responsible for arranging supervisions and generally making sure the student is meeting the university's academic requirements.

A dean of chapel, sometimes assisted by the chaplain, has the college's spiritual welfare at heart while the dean of college is responsible for discipline, a task sometimes shared with the Senior Tutor. Last, but by no means least, is the steward, responsible for organising food and drink.

How the university works

As we have seen, the university is self-governing. In theory it is a huge democracy because the Senate is composed of all living holders of an MA (Master of Arts) degree from Cambridge throughout the world who are entitled to vote on important matters and is, in theory, the ultimate authority.

However, legislative matters are normally referred to the Regent House, composed of the teaching and administrative staff of the university who hold the MA degree. Meetings of the Senate (*not* attended by all the members) and the Regent House are held in the Senate House fifteen times a year and are known as Congregations. Members may vote on motions, known as Graces, which are put before them on these occasions.

The main administrative body of the university is the Council of the Senate with sixteen members elected from the Regent House plus the Vice-Chancellor. All of the university's legislative business which needs the assent of the Regent House is prepared by the Council.

Peterhouse

The Vice-Chancellor, appointed for a maximum of seven years, is the principal officer of the university, is chairman of the Council of the Senate and of the General Board of the Faculties which advises the university on educational policy and ensures that the necessary resources are available to maintain high standards of teaching and research. Many of its proposals also have to be ratified by the Regent House.

The Financial Board, also chaired by the Vice-Chancellor, controls investments, organises the university budget and maintains buildings.

Academically, the faculties, syndicates and departments, responsible for teaching and research, are supervised by the Councils of the Schools and the Inter-Faculty Committee, both of which report back to the General Board of the Faculties.

All the members of these bodies are elected and will almost certainly also be members of the teaching or administrative staff of the university and/or the colleges.

The University of Cambridge — its history

Until the early nineteenth century England had but two universities, Oxford and Cambridge. Although Cambridge can claim an older civic pedigree than Oxford, the latter, much to the gentle, but continuing, chagrin of Cambridge, is undoubtedly the older university. By how many years is unclear. But what is clear is that in 1209 the students and townspeople of Oxford were in open conflict, some students being killed.

Many migrated to the small but prosperous town of Cambridge. By 1226 they were numerous enough and so well organised as to have set themselves up under an official called a 'chancellor', and to have arranged a series of regular academic courses. This was no mean group of scholars because by 1231 the King had taken them under his protection. He ordained they were not to be exploited by their landlords and insisted that only those enrolled for tuition under a recognised 'Master' should be allowed to stay in the town. This was important – it meant that the Masters had a monopoly of teaching.

Documents discovered recently in the Vatican library have proved to be statutes of the University of Cambridge of about 1250 and show Cambridge to have been one of the twenty *Studia Generale* in existence in Europe before 1300, although Cambridge had to wait until 1318 for formal recognition by Pope John XXII as a *Studium Generale*. Already at that time there was a common pattern of study in Europe which had also been known at Oxford and to those who were flocking to Cambridge. It consisted of a foundation course lasting three years during which students 'read' Latin grammar, logic and rhetoric (the *Trivium*), followed by four years studying arithmetic, music, geometry and astronomy (the *Quadrivium*). These courses led to the degrees of bachelor and master.

Early students – not to be confused with younger 'undergraduates' of later centuries – were mainly clerics or clerks in some form of holy orders. Statutes of Peterhouse, the first of the colleges (founded 1284) tell us about the appearance of its members in 1338: ' The Master, and all and each of the Scholars of our house, shall adopt the clerical dress and tonsure and not allow their beard or their hair to grow contrary to canonical prohibition nor wear rings upon their fingers for their vainglory and boasting.'

Early teaching

Early teaching was done by the reading and explaining of texts by Masters who had themselves passed through the course. Examinations were oral; students disputed a series of questions with the Masters.

Masters who wished to progress entered into advanced studies in divinity, law, medicine and music, again being taught by others who had themselves passed this particular course. They then became 'doctors' and formed themselves into different faculties.

To bring order to the system it became necessary to identify and register those who sought to obtain degrees. Enrollment with a licensed Master became known as 'matriculation' – the student's name had to be on the Master's roll or *matriculus*. As the student progressed he was admitted to different grades of membership of the university. In other words he 'graduated'. Commonly throughout Europe different grades of scholars were marked by variations in their academical dress of gown, hood and cap.

Apart from having a chancellor the Regent Masters – the teaching body – realised they needed other officials to regulate their affairs. First they elected two proctors to supervise ceremonies, to negotiate with outside bodies, to guard the treasure and to keep records. Later a chaplain took charge of treasure and books, bedells presided over ceremonies, a registry recorded matriculations and admissions to degrees and minuted the meetings of the Regent Masters while an orator wrote ceremonial letters and addresses. These officials still play important roles in the modern university.

Royal patronage

From the earliest times royalty recognised Cambridge's burgeoning importance and cosseted the university conferring upon it privileges which were to infuriate the townspeople until well into the nineteenth century.

The Crown prevented scholars from being exploited by town landlords overcharging for rents. This did not stop the town from raising the prices of food and fuel. Again the Crown intervened, and the university was given the right to proceed in law against profiteers and to enforce the proper sale of bread and ale by the town.

So furious were the citizens that they rioted in 1381 – there had been a previous outburst of violence in 1261 when sixteen townsmen were hanged while twenty-eight scholars were given the King's pardon – destroying university property. This time they were to live to regret it for the Crown further increased the university's privileges by granting to the Chancellor powers to prosecute not only the profiteers but also any townsman who falsified weights and measures, adulterated food and drink, interrupted the supply of fresh water or wilfully introduced infection during bouts of the plague.

Further, the Chancellor was granted jurisdiction over lawsuits occurring during fairs and markets. In addition, the university gradually rid itself of the

Old Schools

dominance of the Bishop of Ely, and before the end of the fifteenth century the only ecclesiastical authority they recognised was that of the Pope. Indeed, the Chancellor became an ecclesiastical judge in his own right, which permitted him to try all cases involving scholars' morals and discipline and to prove wills. These privileges were added to those which already allowed the Chancellor to provide scholars with a secular court in which they could resolve all civil and criminal cases except those involving major crimes. The temptation to abuse such privileges was enormous.

Living-quarters for scholars became an immediate problem. Recognising it, Hugh de Balsham, Bishop of Ely, founded the first college, Peterhouse, in 1284, and Regent Masters banded together to buy or rent large premises called hostels where teaching could take place and lodgings be found. Although these hostels were to continue into the sixteenth century, it was the increasingly rapid foundation of colleges which was to influence the development of the university.

However, the colleges were not founded originally to house youthful undergraduates but to provide accommodation and teaching for small numbers of scholars advanced in the study of law or divinity. King's Hall, later incorporated into Trinity College, was founded by Edward II specifically to produce members of the higher civil service, for example.

Meanwhile, the university was beginning to buy land and to build for itself. As college building continued apace so, in the late fourteenth century, the university acquired property on Senate House Hill. The set of buildings now known as the Old Schools grew up there and housed the more senior faculties. Lectures and disputations were held there, and the university treasure was there with its chests and its muniments as were a library and chapel.

The dissolution of the smaller religious houses gradually led to the provision of facilities for younger students. As more colleges were built — five in the fourteenth century, six in the fifteenth century and a further six in the sixteenth century — they came to play a highly important role in university life. By the middle of the sixteenth century a new advisory council called the Caput was formed consisting of the Chancellor, senior doctors and, significantly, heads of colleges.

Influence of women

Although women were not to be admitted to full membership of the university until 1947, they were to play highly important roles in its development and that of the colleges. Lady Elizabeth of Clare refounded University Hall as Clare Hall, now Clare College; Marie St Pol de Valence, the widowed Countess of Pembroke, founded Pembroke College; two queens, Margaret of Anjou, wife of Henry VI and Elizabeth of Woodville, wife of Edward IV, refounded Queens' College; and later Lady Frances Sidney, Countess of Sussex, was to found Sidney Sussex College. Furthermore, Elizabeth I's statutes for the university of 1570 were to influence it for centuries. They insisted, for example, that all students be members of colleges — that still applies — and that every student, teacher and graduate should attend, as an Anglican, a service in his college chapel every day. That requirement ended only in the late nineteenth century.

Perhaps the most remarkable of these determined ladies was the pious and

Henry VII's arms in King's College Chapel

gentle Lady Margaret Beaufort (1443–1509), mother of Henry VII. We can thank her for the marvellous stone carvings in the west end of King's College Chapel for she persuaded her son to pay for them. She in turn was persuaded by an equally remarkable Cambridge man, John Fisher, to found, first, Christ's College and then, in her will, St John's College. Fisher was her chaplain and he also persuaded the Lady Margaret to found the first endowed university teaching post, the Lady Margaret Chair of Divinity. He was the first to hold the chair in 1503.

This last decision was of enormous importance to the university for it was to be the example which was to trigger so many future benefactions; Henry VIII, for example, was soon to endow five professorial chairs, the Regius Chairs of Divinity, Hebrew, Greek, Physic and Civil Law.

John Fisher — he was Master of Michaelhouse, Proctor, Vice Chancellor and Chancellor in Cambridge before becoming Bishop of Rochester — zealously promoted the New Learning in Greek and Hebrew and encouraged those thinkers to come to Cambridge who, like Erasmus, were to prepare men for the Reformation which in turn would lead to the Dissolution of the Monasteries with all that that was to mean to Cambridge. As an old man he was tried for denying the King's succession and beheaded in 1535. He was canonised in 1935.

The sixteenth century

The sixteenth century was to see more dramatic changes in Cambridge. No longer did colleges attract men destined to be trained solely for the priesthood. Lay scholars began to appear, at Trinity College in particular. The student body was changing its character. Subject matter, too, was changing. Henry VIII, who had founded Trinity in 1546 at the very end of his tumultuous life, had earlier forbidden the study of the canon law and scholastic philosophy in Cambridge. So the study of law was largely replaced by Greek and Latin biblical studies and especially by mathematics. Royal intervention continued for successive monarchs were anxious for the two Universities to produce leaders of the reformed Church. More and more they removed power from the Regent Masters and concentrated it in the hands of the Vice-Chancellor and the Caput.

As the sixteenth century progressed into the seventeenth, the university moved steadily towards an increasing study of mathematics and associated scientific subjects. More chairs were established both by the university and by private benefactors: mathematics, chemistry, astronomy, anatomy, botany, geology, astronomy and geometry, experimental philosophy and mineralogy. Undoubtedly, so far as the future was concerned, the most important of these was the Lucasian Professorship of Mathematics. This was the chair into which Isaac Newton was elected in 1669 when he was just twenty-seven and was to hold for thirty-three glorious years. It has been said that if Cambridge had produced only one student — Newton — in its entire history the effort would have been worthwhile for without his genius the twentieth century as we know it could not have happened.

Although new disciplines were being catered for by the addition of new chairs for

Arabic, moral philosophy, music, modern history and law, Cambridge was dominated by mathematics. It was to be a compulsory subject for all students from 1750 to 1850. Mathematics was *the* examination.

Change came slowly at first with the introduction of the civil law degree of LLB (Bachelor of Laws) in 1816, a classical tripos in 1824 and a theological tripos in the 1840s. Cambridge University Press increased in stature and influence as did the University Library which had outgrown its ancient home in the Old Schools and had moved into sumptuous quarters in the newly built Senate House (1730). The Botanic Garden was now well established behind Free School Lane, and the university had an observatory.

Demand for reform

Demand for change and reform was deafening in the first half of the nineteenth century. The call was answered by the election in 1847 of the Prince Consort as Chancellor, which was followed three years later by the appointment of a Royal Commission into the two ancient universities. The resulting Cambridge University Act of 1856 established a framework of government which still exists today. Expansion of new studies after the Commission was almost meteoric. Natural and moral sciences, oriental and modern and medieval languages and mechanical sciences were all introduced. The Botanic Garden moved to Hills Road, which left a large central area free for development by the university. Onto the site came the great Cavendish Laboratory, departments of medicine, chemistry, zoology and anatomy. Nearby laboratories and museums for

botany, geology, agriculture, physiology and archaeology and anthropology were created.

In the midst of this frantic academic activity, Parliament passed the Cambridge Award Act of 1856 to end centuries of 'town-gown' friction. No longer did the Town Council have to swear to uphold the privileges and liberties of the university, no longer could the Vice-Chancellor grant ale-house licences or supervise weights and measures and the running of markets and fairs. The right of the university to settle legal actions involving a member of the university before the Chancellor's Court was abolished. Even the university's right to arrest 'common women' was finally abandoned in 1894 after an embarrassing case of wrongful conviction.

Changes

Although two colleges for women were established — Girton in 1869 and Newnham in 1872 — women were not to achieve full membership of the university until 1947 and were not to be admitted to previously all-male colleges until the 1970s and after. Today, of the thirty-one colleges, all are co-educational except Newnham and New Hall (1954) and Lucy Cavendish (1965), which are reserved for women students. As the first women's colleges were being founded, the religious qualifications for students were abolished — they no longer had to be communicant members of the Anglican Church or to attend chapel every day. College Fellows were at last allowed to be married without losing their Fellowships. Liberalism flourished and was symbolised by the university's decision in 1873 to establish

Girton College

the University Extension Lecture Programme which sent out lecturers all over England to take university-level education to adults who would otherwise have had no chance of experiencing it. This was the forerunner of the Board of Extramural Studies.

Government grants

As new subjects proliferated, it became clear that the colleges could no longer provide sufficient facilities – scientific and engineering laboratories for example – to maintain their predominance in teaching within the college, so the university was forced to expand its teaching staff and buildings to cope. The first Treasury grant to the university in 1919 came on condition that there was to be another investigative Royal Commission. The result was a recommendation that the university take

over much of the teaching previously carried out by the colleges – and from 1922 all lectures and public teaching were organised by the university. The colleges were still to be responsible for individual teaching in 'supervisions', a responsibility which remains one of the chief glories of Cambridge teaching to this day.

Although Treasury grants continue to be the mainstay of the university's funding, it, like all other such institutions, is required more and more by Government to 'stand on its own feet' and help itself to meet its financial needs. Thus in the modern university commercially tied research is increasingly important, and individual and corporate sponsorship and donations are, naturally, much sought after.

Today more than forty academic disciplines are offered to undergraduates to study. The university and the colleges have come a long way since the *Trivium*.

The Cambridge colleges

Here, in alphabetical order, are the thirty-one colleges in the University of Cambridge, undergraduate and graduate, with their generally accepted dates of foundation, addresses and telephone numbers.

Unless indicated otherwise, all telephone numbers in this guide should be prefixed by the area code 01223 when calling from outside Cambridge.

Christ's College (1505), St Andrew's Street ☎ 334900

Churchill College (1960), Storey's Way ☎ 336000

Clare College (1326), Trinity Lane ☎ 333200

Clare Hall (1966), Herschel Road ☎ 332360

Corpus Christi College (1352), Trumpington Street ☎ 338000

Darwin College (1964), Silver Street ☎ 335660

Downing College (1800), Regent Street ☎ 334800

Emmanuel College (1584), St Andrew's Street ☎ 334200

Fitzwilliam College (1966), Huntingdon Road ☎ 332000

Girton College (1869), Huntingdon Road ☎ 338999

Gonville and Caius College (1348), Trinity Street ☎ 332400

Homerton College (1894), Hills Road ☎ 507111

Hughes Hall (1885), Mortimer Road ☎ 334898

Jesus College (1496), Jesus Lane ☎ 339339

King's College (1441), King's Parade ☎ 331100

Lucy Cavendish College (1965), Lady Margaret Road ☎ 332190

Magdalene College (1542), Magdalene Street ☎ 332100

New Hall (1954), Huntingdon Road ☎ 762100

Newnham College (1871), Sidgwick Avenue ☎ 335700

Pembroke College (1347), Trumpington Street ☎ 338100

Peterhouse (1284), Trumpington Street ☎ 338200

Queens' College (1448), Queens' Lane ☎ 335511

Robinson College (1977), Grange Road ☎ 339100

St Catharine's College (1473), Trumpington Street ☎ 338300

St Edmund's College (1896), Mount Pleasant ☎ 821504

St John's College (1511), St John's Street ☎ 338600

Selwyn College (1882), Grange Road ☎ 335846

Sidney Sussex College (1596), Sidney Street ☎ 338800

Wren Library, Trinity College

Trinity College (1546), Trinity Street
☎ 338400
Trinity Hall (1350), Trinity Lane ☎ 332500
Wolfson College (1965), Barton Road
☎ 335900

The Cambridge colleges – with a concise history

Here, the colleges of the university are listed in the order of their foundation dates.

Peterhouse (1284)

Peterhouse is the oldest college, founded by Hugh de Balsham, Bishop of Ely. Its hall, heavily restored in the 1870s, is the only building to survive from the thirteenth century. The poet Thomas Gray was here (1742–6) as was Henry Cavendish who, in the eighteenth century, measured the density of water and was the first person to weigh the world at six thousand million million million tons. Some other famous alumni are Charles Babbage, inventor of the first mechanical computer, Sir Frank Whittle, inventor of the jet engine and Sir Christopher Cockerell, inventor of the hovercraft.

Clare College (1326)

Originally a poor foundation, Clare was refounded in 1338 by Lady Elizabeth of Clare, widowed three times before she was thirty. Fire destroyed the first building, a replacement became dilapidated and was followed by the present court, finished in 1719, which is said to be 'more like a palace than a college'. Clare men include Hugh Latimer, Protestant reformer burned at the stake by Mary Tudor, Charles

Clare College

Townshend, Chancellor of the Exchequer whose taxes precipitated the American War of Independence and General Cornwallis who lost it.

Pembroke College (1347)

Founded by Marie St Pol de Valence, the widowed Countess of Pembroke (she was said to have been 'maid, wife and widow in one day', her husband dying in a jousting tournament on their wedding day), it has the oldest surviving Gatehouse in Cambridge. The chapel is the first completed work of Sir Christopher Wren (1665). Beside the Library is a statue of William Pitt the Younger who came up to Pembroke as a boy of fourteen in 1773 and who became Prime Minister at twenty-four.

Gonville and Caius College (1348)

Established first by Edmund Gonville and re-founded by John Kees (Latinised as Caius) in 1557, it has always had a strong medical tradition. Dr Caius introduced the study of practical anatomy into England and William Harvey, who came up in 1593, discovered the circulation of the blood. The college has three Gates symbolising the academic path along which the student progresses – starting with the Gate of Humility, then the Gate of Virtue and ending with the Gate of Honour.

Trinity Hall (1350)

The 'lawyers college' – it was founded by William Bateman, Bishop of Norwich, whose diocese lost 700 priests in the Black Death. He urgently needed a college to teach men the civil and canon law to replace them. Its chapel is the smallest in Cambridge and the Elizabethan library is little changed. Old 'Hall' men include Lord

Gate of Honour, Gonville and Caius College

Howard of Effingham, the admiral whose fleet defeated the Spanish Armada, poet Robert Herrick ('Gather ye rosebuds while ye may') and author J.B. Priestley.

Corpus Christi College (1352)

Unique in Oxford and Cambridge in that it was founded by the townspeople, members of the guilds of Corpus Christi and the Blessed Virgin Mary. It has the oldest court in Cambridge, and its library has a superb collection of rare books and manuscripts thanks to Matthew Parker, Master from 1544 to 1553, who rescued many from destruction after the Dissolution of the Monasteries. Parker, a man of inquisitive nature, gives us the term 'Nosey Parker'.

President's Lodge in Queens' College's Cloister Court

Elizabethan dramatists John Fletcher and Christopher Marlowe were students here.

King's College (1441)
Henry VI's foundation is described separately and at length on pages 94–101.

Queens' College (1448)
Margaret of Anjou, wife of Henry VI, refounded an earlier, poorer college of 1446. Another queen, Elizabeth of Woodville, wife of Edward IV, became patroness in 1465. The involvement of the two queens gives the college its spelling with the apostrophe following the 's'. Old Court is an unaltered example of medieval brickwork, Cloister Court contains the superb sixteenth-century President's Lodge. Erasmus's Tower is where the great scholar lived and worked between 1510 and 1514. The wooden Mathematical Bridge over the Cam, built in 1905, is the third similar bridge to be constructed.

St Catharine's College (1473)
This college is named after Catharine of Alexandria. She was condemned to be crucified on a wheel, but it miraculously broke when she touched it. The catharine-wheel firework is also named after her. Cambridge's youngest undergraduate, William Wotton, born 1666, knew Latin, Greek and Hebrew when he was six and came up to St Catherine's aged nine. John Addenbrooke read medicine here in the 1690s and left £4,500 on his death in 1719 to found the world-famous Addenbrooke's Hospital.

Jesus College (1496)

On the site of a twelfth-century Benedictine nunnery, Jesus College Chapel is the oldest building in any Cambridge college, and the hall above the kitchens, once the nuns' refectory, has been used continuously as a dining-chamber for over 800 years. The chapel has a memorial to Thomas Cranmer, a Jesus undergraduate, later Fellow and first Protestant Archbishop of Canterbury. He was burned at the stake by Mary Tudor in 1556. Another memorial is to Samuel Taylor Coleridge who came up in 1791. HRH Prince Edward is a Jesus graduate.

Christ's College (1505)

Its foundress was Lady Margaret Beaufort, mother of Henry VII, and her statue above the gate shows her holding a bible. Her coat of arms on the gate and above the door to the Master's Lodge is supported by mythical yales, which are also on the gate of St John's College, her second foundation. God's-house, an earlier college, was moved from its site by the river when Henry VI decided to build King's College there. God's-house became Christ's College on 1 May 1505 when its new charter was granted. New Court, designed by Sir Denys Lasdun in 1966 is dramatically modern. John Milton and Charles Darwin were both students here.

St John's College

Although Lady Margaret Beaufort died in 1509 she had made arrangements for the foundation of a college on the site of a thirteenth-century hospital run by the Monks of St John, and the college's charter was granted on 9 April 1511. The figure on

St John's College from the Backs

the gate-tower is of St John the Evangelist. The college is built in a series of courts moving in time from the Tudor First Court, the Second and Third courts, through the Gothic Revival New Court (1824) to the modern (1967) Cripps Court. Standing on both sides of the river, the college is linked by the Bridge of Sighs. The college boat club challenged Oxford to a race in 1829 and so started the annual University Boat Race on the Thames. Poet William Wordsworth was here as was the slavery abolitionist William Wilberforce.

Magdalene College (1542)

Pronounced 'Maudlin', the college was founded by Henry VIII's Lord Chancellor, Thomas, Baron Audley of Walden, whose descendants still have the right to appoint the new Master. In Second Court stands the Pepys Building which houses the entire library left by Samuel Pepys when he died

Emmanuel College's Front Court

Henry VIII – Trinity College

in 1703, first to his nephew and then to his old college. There are 3,000 volumes, and Pepys' bequest insisted that no books be removed from or added to it. The collection includes his famous diary. A former Master, A.E. Benson, wrote the words of 'Land of Hope and Glory', and George Mallory, who died a few feet from the summit of Mount Everest in 1924, was here.

Trinity College (1546)

The largest of the Oxbridge colleges, Trinity was founded by Henry VIII just before his death. He amalgamated two earlier colleges and endowed the new one magnificently. His statue is on the Great Gate, holding a chairleg in his right hand placed there by prankster students who removed his sceptre. The Great Court covers over 2 acres *0.8 ha*, and traditionally students try to run round it while the clock is striking 12 (it strikes the hours twice) — 380 yards *347.5 m* in 43 seconds. Trinity has nurtured many great intellectuals and has produced thirty-one Nobel Prize-winners. The greatest of Trinity's — of Cambridge's — students was Isaac Newton who came up in 1661. His statue, with those of Francis Bacon, Alfred, Lord Tennyson and other Trinity men, is in the ante-chapel. Lord Byron's statue is in the magnificent Wren Library. Lord Rutherford, whose team split the atom, was here, and HRH the Prince of Wales is a Trinity man.

Emmanuel College (1584)

Sir Walter Mildmay, Chancellor of the Exchequer to Elizabeth I and a man of strong Puritan sympathies, paid £550 for the site which was formerly a Dominican friary, and the college was founded in 1584. The founder was present at the feast of dedication in 1588 when the meal included 'venison from two does, and a cragg of sturgeon'. The chapel, finished in 1677, is by Wren, and the Brick Building was built in 1633 when John Harvard was an undergraduate. Five years later he died of consumption in New England, leaving half his estate and 320 books to found a 'schoale at Newetone'. It became America's first university — Harvard.

Sidney Sussex College (1596)

This is another college founded on the site of an ancient religious order — a Franciscan friary — with money left by Lady Frances Sidney, Countess of Sussex. Childless, the Countess's will insisted that 'such learned persons who receive their Breeding in her Foundation may be termed her issue'. On 23 April 1616, the day Shakespeare died, young Oliver Cromwell enrolled at the college as an undergraduate but left after a year to support his family following his father's death. His head was buried in 1960 in a secret place in the ante-chapel.

Downing College (1800)

After Sidney Sussex no new college was built in Cambridge for nearly 200 years until Sir George Downing founded Downing after many years of legal battles over the family estate. Its first architect, William Wilkins, adopted a neo-Grecian style, and the college has continued to build in the classical tradition. Its new and splendid library is a perfect example.

Girton College (1869)

The first women's college in Cambridge, Girton was founded not here but in Hitchin by Emily Davies. It was inconvenient for Cambridge lecturers to travel so far, so the fledgling college was transferred to Girton, 2^1/$_2$ miles *4 km* north of the city centre — 'near enough for male lecturers to visit but far enough away to discourage male students from doing the same'. Girton is now co-educational having admitted male students 110 years after its foundation.

Newnham College (1871)

The college had modest beginnings in 1871 when lodgings for five women were provided in Regent Street. Newnham Hall was opened on the present site in 1875, and Anne Jemima Clough was appointed

Downing College

Principal. Cambridge's second women's college was designed with warm, red-brick buildings in the William-and-Mary style, and the first college building in Cambridge to be designed by a woman is Newnham's Fawcett Building by Elizabeth Whitworth Scott (1938). Newnham still admits only women.

Selwyn College (1882)

George Augustus Selwyn rowed in the Cambridge crew in the first Varsity Boat Race in 1829 and became the first Bishop of New Zealand. When he died in 1878 it was decided a new Cambridge college would be a fitting memorial to him. The first undergraduates arrived in 1882, and women were admitted in 1976.

Hughes Hall (1885)

The oldest and one of the smallest of the exclusively graduate colleges, Hughes Hall was established as the Cambridge Training college for Women but has admitted men and women equally since 1970. About half its students read for the Postgraduate Certificate in Education.

Homerton College (1894)

One of the best-known teacher-training colleges, Homerton started life in Middlesex but moved to its present site in 1894. Then there were 100 rooms for women students and thirty-eight for men. Three years later the Department of Education insisted they stopped admitting men. They were not to be readmitted until 1978.

St Edmund's College (1896)

The 15th Duke of Norfolk founded the college for the education of Roman Catholic clergy and laity. In 1952 it was opened to laymen and in 1965 became one of Cambridge's new graduate colleges.

New Hall (1954)

The desperate shortage of university places for women students following the Second World War led to the foundation in 1954 of New Hall with sixteen undergraduates and two senior members. At first they were housed in the Hermitage, now part of Darwin College. Donations from the Wolfson Foundation and later the Elizabeth Nuffield Foundation allowed building-work to start on the college's present site, and Queen Elizabeth the Queen Mother opened the college officially on 5 June 1965. Like Newnham, New Hall admits only women students.

Churchill College (1960)

The college is the British and Commonwealth memorial to Sir Winston Churchill, whose own vision inspired its creation. Following a visit to the Massachusetts Institute of Technology in 1955, he determined to found an institution in Britain to train scientists and to encourage universities and industry to work together. An appeal raised £5m, timber for the building was given by Commonwealth countries, and the college received its charter in 1960, with full collegiate status in 1966. Sir Winston wanted seventy per cent of the students to study natural sciences, mathematics or engineering and one third were to be postgraduates. Churchill College was Cambridge's first major work of modern architecture and in 1972 became the first Cambridge male college to admit women. In 1992 the Møller Centre for Continuing Education was opened in the college grounds.

Darwin College (1964)
After the Second World War, Cambridge rapidly realised that a new, wholly graduate college was urgently needed, and in 1963 three colleges – Gonville and Caius, Trinity and St John's – announced their intention of forming one. It was to be housed in the former home of a member of the Darwin family.

Lucy Cavendish College (1965)
Named after the widow of Lord Frederick Cavendish, assassinated in Dublin in 1882, the college is unique in Europe in that it was founded to enable mature women to read for the whole range of university degrees, certificates and diplomas. It now also admits undergraduate women aged twenty-five and over and affiliated students who are graduates of other universities.

Wolfson College (1965)
Cambridge University founded University College in 1965 to provide accommodation

Robinson College

and social facilities for some of the increasing number of graduates flocking to Cambridge from other universities. In 1973 it changed its name in recognition of a major benefaction from the Wolfson Foundation, which provided additional buildings and capital endowment. It caters for both men and women graduates.

Clare Hall (1966)

Clare College founded this postgraduate society which admits men and women graduates. Complete families, including children, share the residential life of Clare Hall.

Fitzwilliam College (1966)

The college grew out of an institution which became the home of non-collegiate students in Cambridge, students who could not afford membership of an established college. Fitzwilliam House, as it was, decided to seek collegiate status, funds were accumulated in the 1960s and its first new buildings were opened in 1963. Fitzwilliam House was granted its charter in 1966 and Fitzwilliam College was born. Its buildings are strikingly modern, and its architecture has been described as 'a riot of sculptural invention'.

Robinson College (1977)

This, the last of the collegiate foundations in Cambridge, was the gift of one man, Mr (later Sir) David Robinson, a self-made millionaire. He gave the university £17m to found a college in his name, and on the day of the official opening by The Queen in 1981, he gave another £1m. A local boy who started work in his father's bicycle shop, Mr Robinson went into television retailing and made millions from his business, Robinson Rentals. His college is the only one in Cambridge to have been founded for graduates and undergraduates of both sexes. The college, its concrete structure is covered by a skin of one and a quarter million handmade Dorset bricks, stands on a beautiful 12-acre *4.9-ha* wooded site.

Theological postgraduate colleges

Cambridge also has theological post-graduate colleges: **Ridley Hall** (1881, Anglican), in Sidgwick Avenue ☎ 741080. Named after Nicholas Ridley, a leader of the English Reformation, the college admits graduates of any university who have studied any subject and intend to take holy orders in the Church of England. **Wescott House** (1881, Anglican), in Jesus Lane ☎ 741000, was founded by Brooke Foss Westcott, Regius Professor of Divinity in Cambridge and later Bishop of Durham. It is now open to members of other universities and also, since 1981, to women. The constitution of the college ensures that it has never become linked with any ecclesiastical party. **Westminster College** (1899, United Reformed Church), in Madingley Road ☎ 741084, trains ministers and was originally founded in London. Westminster is probably the most architecturally interesting of the Cambridge theological colleges. The chapel has excellent modern glasswork designed by Douglas Strachan, and the Senatus Room is one of the finest oak-panelled rooms in Cambridge. **Wesley House** (1925, Methodist), in Jesus Lane ☎ 741033, was originally founded in 1921. The main buildings of red brick and Ancaster stone opened in 1925. The chapel, containing decorative paintings by Harold Speed, dates from 1930. ☐

King's College and King's College Chapel

The Adoration of the Magi by Rubens, 1634

The King's College of Our Lady and St Nicholas in Cambridge was founded in 1441 by the young Lancastrian King of England Henry VI, who was born on 6 December 1421 – St Nicholas' Day. It was to be a modest establishment for a rector and twelve scholars, and building began almost immediately, Henry laying the foundation-stone himself on Passion Sunday.

The year before, at the age of nineteen, Henry had founded a college at Eton, near Windsor, and his college in Cambridge was exclusively for boys from Eton to continue their education. They were awarded degrees without sitting university examinations and were not subject to the authority of the university proctors (Fellows responsible for discipline). Non-Etonians were not admitted to the college until 1873.

The original college court was built north of the chapel. The gatehouse still stands, and the Old Court is now part of the Old Schools, the administrative centre of Cambridge University.

Realising his new college would be too small, Henry revised his plan in 1445. Now the college was to have seventy scholars, and Henry needed more space to build it. His second plan was explained with great detail and clarity in his 'Will' of 12 March 1448. The site he chose was an important part of the medieval town of Cambridge, with houses, mills and wharves by the river and the church and parish of St John Zachary. Milne Street, one of the main thoroughfares of the town, ran through the middle of it. To make room for his college required large-scale demolition and, although Henry bought the site, the townspeople were unhappy with the destruction. The site was cleared but the Wars of the Roses began, Henry was deposed in 1461 and murdered in the Tower of London in 1471 – and the site stood empty for almost 300 years, the college managing in the small buildings of Old Court.

Henry's greatest achievement was the **college chapel**, the last and finest Gothic building to be erected in Europe. As he had

Fan vault

for the college so he laid the foundation-stone for the chapel – white magnesian limestone brought down by boat from quarries in Yorkshire – at the site of the high altar on St James's Day, 25 July 1446. Building began at the east end. On the external walls you can see the white magnesian limestone. When the Yorkshire quarries were worked out, the builders used buff-coloured oolitic limestone from Northamptonshire. The idea was to have walls of glass, so the side-chapels are

Stained glass

tucked underneath the buttresses and there is nothing inside to break the single aisle, reputedly the longest in Europe without any central support. This was a new idea. The interior of the chapel is 289 feet *88.1 m* long, 80 feet *24.4 m* high and 40 feet *12.2 m* wide.

By 1485 the five eastern bays had been built and roofed to form a small chapel. Work continued slowly during the reigns of Edward IV, Edward V and Richard III.

In 1506 King Henry VII and his mother, Lady Margaret Beaufort, came to the small chapel at King's College to attend the St George's Eve service for the Knights of the Garter. Lady Margaret encouraged her son to complete the great work of his predecessor. Henry VII died in 1509 leaving money and instructions for the completion. On 29 July 1515 – sixty-nine years and four

days after Henry VI laid the foundation-stone – the chapel stonework was finished. The stained glass and woodwork had still to be added, and in 1544 the original high altar was erected and this great building was complete. Let us look round it.

It was to have had a lierne vaulted ceiling but John Wastell, the master mason, took the momentous decision to change it to a magnificent **fan vault**, the largest anywhere in the world. Above the fan vault is a 21-foot *6.4-m* space and above that a lead and timber roof. The stone ceiling is estimated to weigh about 1,875 tons, and the large boss in the centre of each section weighs 1 ton. Architect Christopher Wren, on seeing the breathtaking vault for the first time, is reputed to have said that he could have built it – if someone had shown him where to set the first stone!

In 1512, work on the **armorial carvings** in the **ante-chapel** was supervised by Henry VIII's master carver Thomas Stockton. Henry VII's crowned arms are supported by the dragon of Wales (he was a Welshman), and the Richmond greyhound (he was Earl of Richmond before his accession). There is also the crowned Tudor rose, Beaufort portcullis and French fleur-de-lis – all English sovereigns from Edward III to George III claimed they were kings of France. Look carefully at the stone carving; every rose, every dragon, every greyhound is different. The small painted head in the rose left of the west door is said to be the beautiful Princess Elizabeth of York, whose marriage to Henry VII joined the houses of York and Lancaster and ended the Wars of the Roses.

The **stained glass windows** were made between 1517 and 1547 by mainly Flemish glaziers working under Henry VIII's own master glaziers Bernard Flower and Galyon Hone. Henry paid for the windows. Beginning at the north-west corner and continuing clockwise round the chapel, the lower windows show stories from the New Testament and the Apocrypha, starting with the birth of the Virgin Mary, Jesus's birth, childhood, manhood, Crucifixion, Resurrection and Ascension, and ending with the Acts of the Apostles and the Assumption of the Virgin Mary. The upper windows show symbolic parellels taken from the Old

King's College Chapel
from the east

Organ with its carved angels

Testament. For example, above the Entombment of Christ is Joseph being cast into the pit; and above the Resurrection of Christ, Jonah emerging from the whale's mouth. The **east window** is all New Testament and illustrates the story of the Crucifixion. The nineteenth-century **west window** portrays the Day of Judgement with Christ sitting in majesty. Below him St Michael, holding the scales, is deciding who shall be saved and who damned. The young Henry VI can be seen left of centre in the glass at the bottom of the window holding his chapel. During the Second World War all the windows except the west one were removed for the duration.

The **wooden screen** which divides the chapel into ante-chapel and choir was also paid for by Henry VIII. There is no record of who carved the great screen from English oak. However, it is easy to date. On the coving above the central doorway, the initials 'H' 'A', Henry and Anne, are carved in the woodwork and beside it the Boleyn family emblem, a falcon. Further along to the right are the initials 'RA' — *Regina Anne*. Anne Boleyn, Henry's second wife, was Queen from 1533 until her execution in 1536. This is one of only two places where Anne Boleyn is remembered as having been Queen — the other is in Hampton Court .

Thomas Dallam built an **organ** for the chapel in 1605, and the present organ, although mainly seventeenth-century with later additions, still incorporates carving from the Dallam organ. In the eighteenth century the carved angels were replaced with Gothic pinnacles but in 1859 new, trumpeting angels, copied from engravings of the earlier ones, were erected. It is claimed that undergraduates stood up there first to help get the proportions right! The organ has recently been enlarged and rebuilt, and the over 4,000 pipes now fill both organ cases and the screen on which they stand.

Go through the gateway into the **choir**. The **gate** is later than the screen and has the date 1636 and the arms of Charles I. The magnificent **choir stalls** were carved with the screen but Cornelius Austin, a Cambridge craftsman, carved the **canopies** above them from 1675 to 1678. They show the coats of arms of English sovereigns from Henry VI to Charles I and also of Eton and the University of Oxford on the left, or north, side and King's College and the University of Cambridge on the right, or south, side. Oxford has an open book in their arms, Cambridge has a closed one. Oxford says Cambridge is ignorant because their book is always shut; Cambridge says Oxford is lazy because they never turn the page!

The large bronze **lectern** was given to the college in the early sixteenth century by the then Provost (most of the colleges have masters, King's has a provost). On the sloping desks on one side you can read his Christian name 'Robertus', on the other his surname 'Hacumblen'. During services the lectern holds two bibles, the Old Testament is placed on the side with the roses, and the New Testament is put on the other side with the Evangelists and their emblems: St Matthew, a winged man, St Mark, a lion, St Luke, a winged bull, and St John, an eagle. The lectern revolves and the candles swivel so the Bible can be turned to the reader. Henry VI's statue is on the top, and the animals round the bottom are lions, often used to 'guard' the Bible. It was thought they slept with their eyes open so were always watchful – like God.

The choir is Henry VI's end of the chapel. He wanted it to be 'clene and substantial' without 'curious worke of entaille and besy moldyng' so the stone walls at this end are plain. Carved in the stone frieze above the door on your left are four angels, one holding an instrument to represent music, the next a book for learning, a crown for the King and a cross for the church. And notice the lovely ringleted angel beside the door, holding the royal arms of England.

Above the altar is *The Adoration of the Magi*, painted by Peter Paul Rubens in 1634 (see p. 94) for the White Nuns at Louvain in Belgium as an **altarpiece** in their convent chapel. We are told Rubens painted the whole picture in eight days. The beautifully lifelike baby Jesus is said to be a portrait of Rubens' baby son Frans. In 1959 this picture was bought anonymously at auction for £275,000. Two years later the purchaser, Major A.E. Allnatt, gave it to

Choristers in top hats and black gowns

King's College. The magnanimous gift necessitated a major transformation of the chapel.

It was decided the painting should stand above the altar but to ensure it did not obtrude into the great east window the marble floor was lowered. Previously it had risen in steps from the screen to the height of the back of the stone seats set in the wall either side of the altar. While the floor was up, the college installed central heating – 4 miles *6.4 km* of 3-inch *76-mm* copper tubing zigzagging under the floor to keep the picture at the correct temperature. They realised humidifiers were not needed because the thousands of visitors to this chapel every year breathe out sufficient moist air! When the floor was relaid some of the marble squares were renewed. The black marble came from Belgium, while the white is Carrara marble from Italy.

The great **east window** can be divided into seven parts. The top section is full of Tudor initials and emblems; the bottom lights tell the story of the Passion. Starting from the bottom left, the first three lights represent Christ being shown to the people, the central three Pontius Pilate's court with Pilate washing his hands, the right-hand three, Jesus carrying the cross. The upper half left-hand three lights show Jesus being nailed to the Cross, the central three Jesus and the thieves on the crosses, and the right-hand three Jesus being taken down from the Cross.

The red graffiti on the stone walls is thought to have been put there by Oliver Cromwell's soldiers. The Parliamentary Army used the chapel as a drill hall during the Civil War. The carved stone figures either side of the south door are also thought to have been defaced by them.

King's College Choir is famous throughout the world. It is a male choir and – according to the wishes of Henry VI – consists of sixteen choristers (who wear top hats and short black gowns similar to the uniform of Eton when they come to the chapel for choir practice and services) and who attend King's College Choir School and fourteen choral scholars from the college. Since 1928, the Festival of Nine Lessons and Carols on Christmas Eve has been broadcast from here annually. It is heard and seen around the world. The service always starts with the solo voice of a small chorister singing the first verse of 'Once in Royal David's City'. The boy is not told he has been chosen to sing until just before the service starts. During term, the choir sings Evensong every day except Monday, and visitors are welcome to attend the service.

Services are performed by candlelight – but candles smoke, dirtying the stone walls. After the great cleaning and alterations to the chapel in the 1960s following the gift of the Rubens painting, it was decided to burn smokeless candles from Lilleholmen in Sweden to keep the walls clean.

Do go into the **chapel exhibition** through the north door in the choir. It will tell you more about the history of this great building and of the scholars and craftsmen who created it.

Leaving the chapel, go into **Front Court** and look first at the chapel walls. Notice the white magnesian limestone at the east end and the buff-coloured oolitic limestone which was used when the quarries in Tadcaster, Yorkshire, had no more stone. Notice also the buttresses. The ones at the east end are plain. That is Henry VI's end – he wanted a simple chapel. The buttresses at the west end have statues on them. This is Henry VII's end. He loved carving and was responsible for all the Tudor stone embellishments in the ante-chapel.

Front Court was the centre of the medieval town which Henry VI destroyed to build his college and chapel. It stood empty for almost 300 years until James Gibbs was asked to produce plans for three sides of a court, and in 1724 the foundation-stone of the **Gibbs' Fellows' Building** was laid. It was a highly unusual foundation-stone. An enormous stone with a deep cut in it had lain beside the chapel for many years. Workmen were said to be actually sawing it in half when news reached them that Henry VI had been deposed. They threw down their tools and immediately stopped work.

In the 1820s the college held a competition offering £600 for a design to complete Front Court. William Wilkins won. He designed the neo-Gothic **screen** and **gatehouse** that separates the court from King's Parade and the south range which includes the **dining-hall** with two oriel windows, the **library** and the old **Provost's lodge**. The statue of Henry VI holding his 'will and intente' was placed here in 1879. Sometimes Henry looks quite different. If the weather is wet he might be wearing a flat cap or a college scarf and at Hallowe'en he has been seen with a pumpkin! And the fountain has been filled with washing-up liquid with bubbles floating gently round the court. The figures on the fountain represent Learning, holding a book, and Religion, holding the chapel.

Walk round to the west end of the chapel. The land over the river called **Scholars' Piece** belongs to King's College and often has sheep or cattle grazing on it. This is part of the famous **Backs** of Cambridge, called so simply because here are the backs of the six riverside colleges. They used to be called Backsides.

Look at the west end of the chapel with its newly restored stonework. This is the famous view shown on so many Christmas cards and photographs of Cambridge — the wonderful Gothic Perpendicular building with pierced battlements and soaring turrets decorated with crowned Tudor roses and Beaufort portcullises. Sometimes the chapel turrets have different decorations — chamber-pots, under-garments, even notices put there by the night-climbing students of Cambridge.

In 1615 Henry Man was paid just over £22 for the great oak **west door**. The wooden carving at the top has a sun inscribed with the word 'Jahveh' in Hebrew characters, palm-trees, lilies, two cherub heads and roses. The niches either side of the doorway were for statues of the Virgin Mary and St Nicholas, but never placed.

If you are following one of our walks, please leave the college through the gate by which you entered and rejoin the walk. □

Services

Choral Evensong daily in term-time Mon–Sat 1730 (on Mon the singers are King's Voices, Tue–Sat King's College Choir, Wed men's voices only, Fri unaccompanied by the organ). Sun services 1030 and 1530, but on the first Sun of the month Evensong is at 1800. Please check with Cambridge Tourist Information Centre (01223) 322640 or King's Chapel Services information on (01223) 331155

Churches

*Great St Mary's
church clock*

Cambridge has many fine churches. A number of them served for long periods as worshipping-places for colleges before the colleges built their own chapels. Indeed, early colleges were deliberately sited close to existing churches — like Peterhouse which stood beside St Peter-without-Trumpington-Gate and Corpus Christi beside St Bene't's. Both colleges built galleries connecting the college buildings to the church.

All Saints in the Jewry
The fifteenth-century Church of All Saints in the Jewry stood on St John's Street. The west tower had an open archway with the pavement running underneath it. The street was widened in 1865 and the church demolished. All that remains is its churchyard, now a garden, and a memorial cross commemorating some of the old parishioners. The following year the new Gothic Revival church designed by G.F. Bodley was built in Jesus Lane, opposite the entrance to Jesus College. The spire was not finished until 1871. Three bells

from the old church and various monuments, floor slabs and tablets and the fifteenth-century clunch font with an octagonal bowl were transferred to the new church. The interior was decorated by William Morris with stencilling on the walls and ceiling, and the stained glass windows have work by William Morris, Burne-Jones, Ford Maddox Brown and C.E. Kempe. The church, no longer used for services, is in a poor state of repair. The key is available, on payment of £3.50 returnable deposit, from 'Every Occasion', 84 King Street ☎ 576500.

St Andrew the Great

The Church of St Andrew the Great, which stands on St Andrew's Street opposite the entrance to Christ's College, was built on the site of an earlier church, St Andrew-without-Barnwell-Gate, demolished in 1842. Rebuilding started in the same year. Architect Ambrose Poynter designed a simple late fifteenth-century Gothic style church with no division between the nave and sanctuary and no clerestory. The west tower is of four stages with an embattled parapet. On the north wall in the sanctuary is a memorial to navigator Captain James Cook, killed by natives of Hawaii in 1779 and to six of his children who all had tragic deaths – two were lost at sea, one died whilst an undergraduate at Christ's College and the other three died in infancy. His wife Elizabeth and their two surviving sons are buried in the nave. For a number of years the Church of St Andrew was empty and neglected. In the early 1990s, renovation began, and in March 1994 services recommenced. St Andrew's is now used by the congregation of the Round Church, who found that their small church could no longer house their large and congregation.

Saxon tower of St Bene't's Church

St Andrew the Less

The Church of St Andrew the Less, also known as the Abbey Church, is on Newmarket Road, close to the roundabout and the Elizabeth Bridge. It is known as the abbey church because it belonged to the Augustinian Barnwell Priory founded in the early twelfth century, which was the largest and most important of all the religious houses in Cambridge. The walls are of clunch rubble, extensively refaced. Built in the early thirteenth century, it has only a chancel and a nave. The east wall has three thirteenth-century lancet windows, and the south doorway is largely original. The vestry and organ chamber were added in the nineteenth century, and the south porch was built in 1929 on the site of an earlier one.

St Bene't

St Bene't's Church, tucked away in Bene't Street which leads off King's Parade, is dedicated to St Benedict. The tower is the oldest building in the county, built about

1025 during the reign of the Danish King Canute (Cnut). The tapering tower, made of rubble with 'long and short' quoins or cornerstones was built in three stages. The double-headed belfry windows are original as are the circular openings above them. The interior semi-circular tower arch springs from carved lions. Parts of the nave and chancel are also original with later alterations and additions. The nave was rebuilt in the second half of the thirteenth century. The north and south aisles were rebuilt and enlarged in the nineteenth century. The adjoining college of Corpus Christi was founded in 1352 and used part of St Bene't's as their college chapel until they built their own in 1579. There are six bells, the oldest dated 1588. Fabian Stedman, the inventor of change-ringing, was parish clerk here in the 1670s, and these bells probably rang the first organised peal. The church has a seventeenth-century fire-hook and coffin stool and a bible that belonged to Thomas Hobson – of Hobson's choice fame. The eighteenth-century marble font has been reinstated; the nineteenth-century one that temporarily replaced it was given to the cathedral in Halifax, Nova Scotia.

St Botolph

Standing on Trumpington Street at its junction with Silver Street, St Botolph's was just inside the medieval Trumpington Gate on the main road to London. St Botolph, a seventh-century Benedictine abbot from East Anglia, became the patron saint for travellers. Churches dedicated to him were built on the edge of medieval towns, and there you prayed for a good journey before you set off and gave thanks when you arrived safely. The present church was built

about 1320 on the site of an earlier one. The west tower is fifteenth century. At its corners are the emblems of the Evangelists – the lion, ox, man and eagle. The four bells were cast in 1460 and have never been altered. The medieval stone font has a beautiful seventeenth-century wooden octagonal cover and canopy. There are memorials to Robert Grumbold, 1720, and James Essex, 1784, both of whom did much building-work in Cambridge, and to John Smith, the university printer who gave the altarpiece, an eighteenth-century copy of a *Crucifixion* by Van Dyck. The nave is roofed with old, unusual 'fish scale' tiles.

St Clement

St Clement was the Danish saint for seafarers. His church is on Bridge Street near the river where the Viking invaders had their important trading-post in the ninth and tenth centuries. The church was largely rebuilt in the early thirteenth century, and the Early English nave arcades date from this period. In the early sixteenth century the north and south aisles were rebuilt and a clerestory added. The west tower was built in 1821 from a bequest of the Revd William Cole. Carved in the stone above the west door is a pun on his name *Deum Cole* – 'worship God'. His remains are entombed under the centre of the tower.

St Edward King and Martyr

This church in St Edward's Passage, between King's Parade and Peas Hill, is dedicated to the Saxon King Edward the Martyr (963-978), murdered at Corfe Castle by his stepmother. The walls are of stone rubble, much of it cement-rendered. The tower probably dates from the late twelfth century. The fourteenth-century nave has acutely pointed arches, unusual for the period. The chancel was rebuilt in the middle of the fifteenth century, and the north and south chapels were added by Trinity Hall and Clare Hall, later Clare College, to be used as their college chapels when their parish church of St John Zachary was demolished by Henry VI to make way for King's College. St Edward's is closely connected with the early reformers. The sixteenth-century oak pulpit is the one from which Hugh Latimer preached. This pulpit was thrown out in the nineteenth century and bought by the Provost of King's College. King's returned it in 1949 when the Latimer memorial window was installed. A tablet remembers Thomas Bilney 1531, Robert Barnes 1540 and Hugh Latimer 1555, who were all burned to death in the reign of Mary Tudor.

St Giles

The Victorian Church of St Giles on Castle Hill stands on the site of an older church built about 1092 by Lady Hugolina, the wife of Sir Roger Picot, Governor of Cambridge Castle and the first Norman sheriff of Cambridge-shire. Lady Hugolina fell dangerously ill and vowed that if she got better she would build and dedicate a church in honour of her patron saint Giles. Three days later she recovered. She and her husband built the church and brought an Augustinian prior and six canons from Normandy. The canons later moved to a larger, better site at Barnwell where they re-established their priory in 1213. The present St Giles Church was built in 1875 incorporating some parts of the old church, including the chancel arch which now stands between the south aisle and the south chapel.

Holy Sepulchre – Round Church

Holy Sepulchre

The Church of the Holy Sepulchre, or the Round Church as it is always called, standing at the corner of Bridge Street and Round Church Street, is one of the four surviving round churches in England. In the early twelfth century, local members of the Fraternity of the Holy Sepulchre were given land by the Abbot of Ramsey to build a church – a round church to commemorate the Church of the Holy Sepulchre in Jerusalem. They built a circular nave and aisle and a small chancel. In the fifteenth century the little church had a polygonal belfry built above the clerestory of the 'round' or nave, and most of the windows of the round were altered and enlarged. In 1841 the Cambridge Camden Society and their architect Anthony Salvin began a huge restoration, destroying much of the fifteenth-century work. They replaced the bell tower with a conical roof and the old clerestory windows with pseudo-Norman ones, they enlarged the chancel, built a new south aisle and cleaned all the stonework. The Round Church was damaged by a bomb during the Second World War, when the east window was blown out. The new window of 1946 shows Christ crucified on a living tree – the Tree of Life.

Holy Trinity

The Church of the Holy Trinity stands at the corner of Market and Sidney streets. The original twelfth-century church, probably timber framed and thatched, was destroyed in the great fire of 1174 and then rebuilt. Little of the second church remains. In the late fourteenth century the north and south aisles were added – there is a consecration cross on the north wall – and the west tower was built. The tower buttresses and nave clerestory are fifteenth century. The south aisle was widened in the sixteenth century, and in the nineteenth there was more restoration and rebuilding. In the chancel is a monument to Charles Simeon, appointed perpetual curate and lecturer in 1782, who ministered here for fifty-four years. Holy Trinity became the centre of the Cambridge evangelical revival. There is a memorial to Revd Henry Martyn, Fellow of St John's College who translated the New Testament into Hindustani and Persian. The vestry houses a collection of the Revd Charles Simeon's relics, including his 'preaching Bible', his teapot and a large green umbrella – he was one of the first people in the country to use one.

St Mary the Great

Standing on King's Parade between the University Senate House and the market square, the Late Perpendicular Gothic Great St Mary's, as it is affectionately called, has for centuries been the principal church in Cambridge. Uniquely, it has been both spiritual and intellectual centre for it is the university church — documents were kept here, lectures, congregations and degree ceremonies were all held here. Six times each year the University Sermons are still preached here, attracting members of the university wearing their gowns and hoods. It is also the main city church used by the Mayor and Corporation of the City of Cambridge who process here on important civic occasions.

The earliest record of a church on this site dates from 1205 but it is likely there was a much earlier church. On 16 May 1478 'at forty-five minutes past 6 p.m.' the foundation-stone of the new church was

St Mary the Great

laid, work continuing until the completion in 1519. The church bells were rung 'as never before' in 1596 although the tower was not finished until 1608. The external walls are rubble and oolitic limestone, the interior is faced with clunch – local soft limestone. The roof is made of oak timbers given by Henry VII. In 1726 they were tied in to a roof above. All undergraduates and BAs had to attend the University Sermons, and as the university grew more seats were needed. In 1735 James Gibbs designed the galleries – with a raised platform at the east end so the university proctors, responsible for discipline, could control improper behaviour. Most of the Cambridge men who led the Reformation in England preached in Great St Mary's; thirty-five of them were burned to death in the reign of Mary Tudor. During the Reformation all the stained glass was destroyed – a glazier was paid four pence to take down the 'Bishop of Rome's' head – so the glass is all nineteenth century. The clerestory windows show the 'glorious company of the Apostles' – some faces are those of leading Victorian churchmen. The nineteenth-century pulpit can slide to the middle of the church on rails so the preacher of the University Sermon can be seen from both galleries. There are two organs, one belonging to the university, one to the parish. The present pews were installed in 1869, and the gilded *Majestas* of 1959 shows the risen Christ standing before a cross that has sprouted leaves – the Tree of Life. Near the altar is a brass plate to German Lutheran Martin Bucer (or Butzer), buried here in 1552. Mary Tudor had him exhumed, and his coffin was tied to a stake in the market place and burned. In Elizabeth's reign soil from the market

place was put in a coffin and he was 'reburied' in the church.

In the chancel there is a memorial to Dr William Butler, 1618, an eminent medical man who cured his patients of malingering by throwing them into the River Thames! Great St Mary's now has a peal of twelve bells, one of only twenty such in the country. Most of the bells are eighteenth century. The chime on the tower clock of 1793 was copied for Big Ben at Westminster. The circle cut to the right of the outside west door is a datum point. All distances from Cambridge are measured from here. Students previously had to live within 3 miles *4.8 km* of here, Fellows within 10 miles *16 km*.

St Mary the Less

St Mary the Less, or Little St Mary's as it is always called, is half-way down Trumpington Street. The original pre-Conquest church called St Peter-without-Trumpington-Gate was used by the next door college which took the name Peterhouse. The church and college are still connected by a gallery. The original church collapsed and was rebuilt and rededicated in 1352. Underneath the late fourteenth-century vestry is a vaulted ossuary or bone hole which was restored in 1960 and is now a small chapel. The church is wonderfully light and airy with beautiful modern glass entrance doors made by local craftsman Mark Bury in 1981. The words are from a poem by George Herbert, one time Orator for the University of Cambridge. The east window has fine decorated tracery but most of the glass in the church is nineteenth-century. The oak pulpit of 1741 and sounding-board are inlaid with mahogany strips. The font,

St Mary the Less

1632, may have been given by Mathew Wren, uncle of Christopher Wren and Master of Peterhouse. The shields show the symbols of St Peter and the Virgin Mary and the emblems of Peterhouse, the City of Cambridge, the University of Cambridge, the Bishopric of Ely and the City of London. On the wall near the entrance is a memorial to Godfrey Washington, great-uncle of George Washington. The Washington family coat of arms is said to have inspired the flag of the United States — the Stars and Stripes. The lovely churchyard which was laid out as a wild garden in 1926 has many rare and interesting plants and shrubs – a peaceful place to rest on a hot summer's day.

St Mary Magdalene

Heading out of Cambridge along the Newmarket Road, cross a railway-bridge and immediately on the left is the beautiful little Stourbridge Chapel. Built of flint in the twelfth century, it was the chapel of a leper hospital attached to the Barnwell Priory and dedicated to St Mary Magdalene. This is one of the finest examples of Norman architecture in the county and has been little altered. In 1211 King John granted a fair to the lepers of the hospital and this became the famous Stourbridge Fair. After the Dissolution the chapel survived because the fairkeepers used it as a storehouse and also as a stable and a drinking-booth. In 1843 the chapel was restored and used for services for the men building the Eastern Counties Railway. The chapel key is at Station House, the second of the two houses down the drive beside the chapel.

St Michael

St Michael's stands on Trinity Street, opposite the entrance to Gonville and Caius College. An older church on the site was rebuilt in the 1320s in Decorated Gothic style. Hervey de Stanton acquired it to serve his new college of Michaelhouse – called after the church and which was later amalgamated with Trinity College – and Gonville Hall, now Gonville and Caius College. He died in 1327, leaving instructions that the church was to be completed. It has hardly been altered since and has wonderful examples of fourteenth-century work. To provide room for all the college members to attend services, the chancel is much larger than the nave. It was restored in 1849 after a fire. Since 1908 St Michael's has been joined to Great St Mary's and is now used mainly as a centre for meetings, plays, examinations and social gatherings.

Our Lady and the English Martyrs

The Roman Catholic Church of Our Lady and the English Martyrs at the corner of Hills and Lensfield roads was built with money given by Mrs Yolande Marie Louise Lyne-Stephens, a former ballerina. She married the 'richest commoner in England', whose death left her enormously wealthy.

She insisted the entire cost of the church and rectory should be 'borne by her alone', even selling a valuable pearl necklace to help towards the cost. The church, built in neo-Gothic style, celebrated its centenary in 1990. When it was built the 216-foot *65.8-m* spire is the highest landmark in Cambridgeshire. The west window shows the English Martyrs, the clergy with St John Fisher and the laity grouped round St Thomas More. In the high altar are relics of Sts Felix and Constantia, martyrs of the early church. and behind it a painting of the Virgin Mary by Sassoferrato (1605–85). The church was struck by a bomb in the Second World War. There are eight bells – the tenor weighing 32 cwt *1,625 kg* is believed to be the largest in the county – and an angelus bell. The church has an ancient oak statue of the Virgin Mary which may have come from the Dominican friary where Emmanuel College now stands.

St Peter on Castle Hill

This must be one of the smallest churches in the country, the nave measuring only 25 by 16 feet *7.6 by 4.9 m*. The original church was considerably larger but by the 1770s it was in a bad state of repair, and in 1781 everything except the fourteenth-century west tower and spire and the west part of the nave was pulled down and this small church was built using the old materials, including flint rubble and Roman bricks. The nave has a twelfth-century Norman doorway and an early thirteenth-century one. The twelfth-century font has carved stone tritons holding up their double tails to make a loop pattern round the bowl. The key for St Peter's can be obtained from nearby Kettle's Yard during normal opening hours.

Religious denominations

Assemblies of God
Tenison Road Church, Tenison Road ☎ 570848

Baptist
Eden Baptist Church, Fitzroy Street ☎ 361250
Hope Strict Baptist Chapel, Cambridge Place ☎ 248771
Mill Road ☎ 248749
St Andrew's Street ☎ 506343
Zion Baptist Church, East Road ☎ 576385

Buddhist
Cambridge Buddhist Centre, Newmarket Road ☎ 460252

St Peter on Castle Hill

Christadelphian
184 Vinery Road ☎ 01638 507571

Christian Brethren
14 Panton Street ☎ 245584

Christian Scientist
60 Panton Street ☎ 355009

Christian Spiritualist
Thompson's Lane.

Church of England
Christ Church, Newmarket Road ☎ 353794
Great St Mary, Senate House Hill ☎ 350914
Holy Cross, Newmarket Road ☎ 413343
Holy Sepulchre (The Round Church), Bridge
Street ☎ 518218
Holy Trinity, Market Street ☎ 355397
Little St Mary, Trumpington Street ☎ 350733
St Andrew the Great, St Andrew's Street
☎ 518218
St Andrew the Less (The Abbey Church),
Newmarket Road ☎ 353794
St Bene't, Bene't Street ☎ 353903
St Botolph, Trumpington Street ☎ 363529
St Clement, Bridge Street ☎ 363457
St Edward King and Martyr, St Edward's
Passage ☎ 362004
St Giles, Chesterton Road ☎ 361919
St Mark, Barton Road ☎ 363339
St Paul, Hills Road ☎ 354186

Evangelical Presbyterian
Clarkson Road.

Greek Orthodox
St Clement, Bridge Street ☎ 354587

Islam
Cambridge Muslim Welfare Society, Mawson
Road ☎ 350134

Jehovah's Witness
Stanley Road ☎ 211552

Jewish
Hebrew Congregation, Thompson's Lane
☎ 246751

Lutheran (German)
Shaftesbury Road ☎ 356167

Methodist
Castle Street ☎ 356047
Wesley, King Street ☎ 352115

Mormon
Church of Jesus Christ of Latter Day Saints,
670 Cherryhinton Road ☎ 247010

Mount Zion Pentecostal
Meets Chesterton Methodist Church, Green End
Road ☎ 563261

National Spiritualist
Myers Memorial Hall,Thompson's Lane.

Quaker
Society of Friends, 12 Jesus Lane ☎ 357535

Resurrection Lutheran
Resurrection Lutheran Church, 25 Westfield
Lane ☎ 461465

Roman Catholic
Our Lady and the English Martyrs, Hills Road
☎ 350787
St Laurence, Milton Road ☎ 354788
University Roman Catholic Chaplaincy, Fisher
House, Guildhall Street ☎ 350018

Salvation Army
Tenison Road ☎ 367633

Seventh Day Adventist
17 Hobart Road ☎ 570556

Unitarian
Emmanuel Road ☎ 355221

United Reformed
Emmanuel, Trumpington Street ☎ 351174
St Columba's, Downing Street ☎ 314586
Victoria Road ☎ 351943

Others
Cambridge Community Church, 14 Alpha
Terrace ☎ 844415
Castle End Mission, Pound Hill ☎ 367722 ☐

Museums

Greek and Roman statues in the Museum of Classical Archaeology

The overlapping interests of town and gown mean that Cambridge is endowed with a remarkable selection of the very finest museums, ranging from the internationally important Fitzwilliam to the homely and fascinating Folk Museum.

Cambridge and County Folk Museum, 2–3 Castle Street. The Folk Museum is housed in what was a sixteenth-century timber-framed farmhouse – one of the oldest dwelling-houses in Cambridge — which became The White Horse Inn in the seventeenth century. The building itself is fascinating, with winding stairs and small rooms full of exhibits illustrating the work and everyday life of local people over the last 300 years. Topics include domestic life, life in the Fens, trades and industries and childhood. There are workshops and activity days for children.

Admission charge. Open April–Sept Mon–Sat 1030–1700, Sun 1400–1700. Between Oct–March the museum is closed on Mondays, except during school holidays.

Closed Christmas and New Year. Shop. Disabled access is limited, please telephone in advance. There is a taped guide to the ground-floor rooms for the blind and partially sighted. ☎ 355159

Cambridge Darkroom, see below under Galleries

Cambridge University Collection of Air Photographs, The Mond Laboratory, New Museums Site, reached from Free School Lane. The collection has over 400,000 air photographs showing the natural environment and the effects of human activity from prehistoric times to the present day. Members of the public can visit the collection. The photographs cannot be borrowed but can normally be copied for a fee. Copies are made to order and usually take about a month.

Cambridge and County Folk Museum

Admission free. Open Mon–Thu 0900–1300 and 1400–1700 Fri 0900–1300 and 1400–1600. Closed Christmas, Easter, Bank holidays and weekends. Disabled visitors please telephone in advance. ☎ 334578

Cambridge University Museum of Archaeology and Anthropology, Downing Street. Many of the exhibits were collected by students and staff of the museum and the faculty in the course of their research. The Gallery of World Prehistory traces mankind's development from the earliest times to the start of literate civilisation, continuing for the Cambridge region into post-medieval times. There are displays of local antiquities and an exhibition of art and culture from many regions of the world.

Admission free. Open Tue–Sat 1400–1630, closed Sun and Mon. Opening hours may be extended from 1030 to 1630 from mid-June to Sept. Schools and large groups by appointment. Shop. Disabled access, please telephone in advance. ☎ 333516

Cambridge University Museum of Classical Archaeology, Sidgwick Avenue. The museum, housed in a new purpose-built gallery, contains one of the largest and finest collections of plaster casts of Greek and Roman sculpture in the world, comprising over 600 works.

Admission free. Open Mon–Fri 0900–1700. Postcards and catalogues on sale. For disabled access please telephone in advance. Groups must book in advance. ☎ 335153

Cambridge Museum of Technology, Cheddars Lane. The museum was formerly a Victorian sewage pumping-station on

Fitzwilliam Museum

Riverside. Steam is raised on a hand-fired Babcock and Wilcox boiler, believed to be the oldest land-based water-tube boiler still regularly steamed. There are steam, gas and electric pumping-engines, including the original boiler plant designed to burn city refuse to raise steam, as well as examples of local industry – hand-operated and powered letter-presses from the 1840s, radios and other electrical equipment.

There is an admission charge, which is higher when steaming takes place. Open 1400–1700 on the first Sunday of each month and from Easter to November open every Sunday. Also open for Steam events. Special visits by appointment. Shop.

Disabled access, please telephone in advance. ☎ 368650

Cambridge University Museum of Zoology, Downing Street. Housed in a light, spacious modern building, the museum has a spectacular survey of the animal kingdom, including corals, marine invertebrates, exotic birds, mammal skeletons, insects and fossil specimens of extinct mammals that are still used for teaching and research. Some of the material was collected by well-known naturalists, including Charles Darwin who donated specimens from his voyage on the Beagle.

Admission free. Children must be accompanied by an adult. Open Mon–Fri in university term-time 1400–1645. Other times Mon–Fri 1000–1300. School parties at other times by appointment. Closed Christmas, Easter and Bank Holidays. Disabled access if one step at the entrance can be negotiated. Lift between floors on request. ☎ 336650

Fitzwilliam Museum, Trumpington Street. The Fitzwilliam Museum is named after the 7th Viscount Fitzwilliam whose collections, bequeathed to his old university in 1816, form the nucleus of this magnificent treasure-house. Work on the building began in 1837 but architect George Basevi never saw the completion. He was inspecting work on the top of Ely Cathedral's west tower, stepped back and fell to his death. The superb marble and mosaic entrance-hall was designed by E.M. Barry. The Fitzwilliam was one of Britain's earliest public picture galleries and now has an internationally famous collection of paintings, drawings and prints from the early Italian school to the present day, with a superb gallery of miniatures. There are

Scott Polar Research Institute

Egyptian, Greek, Roman and West Asiatic antiquities, glass, sculpture, silver, textiles, furniture, coins and medals, clocks, armour, an outstanding display of ceramics and a collection of fans, as well as illuminated musical and literary manuscripts and rare books. The permanent displays are supplemented by temporary exhibitions.

Admission free. Open Tue–Sat 1000–1700; Sun 1415-1700. Also open on some Bank holidays. Closed Mon and over Christmas and New Year. Guided tours Sun 1430 or by arrangement. Shop, coffee bar. Disabled access using signposted rear entrance. ☎ 332900

Kettle's Yard, entrances on Northampton and Castle streets. Kettle's Yard is a museum and a gallery. It was the home of Jim and Helen Ede who befriended and encouraged young aspiring artists and helped them financially by buying their pictures. In 1966 the Edes gave their home and collections to the University of Cambridge. Their house is kept as it was when they lived there, with their collection of early twentieth-century pictures and sculpture, their ceramics and furniture and small objects they collected on their travels. Nothing is behind glass, nothing is numbered or explained. The house collection includes works by Henri Gaudier-Brzeska, Winifred Nicholson, Barbara Hepworth, Henry Moore, David Jones, Ben Nicholson, Christopher Wood, Alfred Wallis, Lucie Rie and others. In 1970 an extension and temporary exhibitions gallery was added to house a changing collection of international contemporary art.

Admission free. Open: House Easter–Aug Tue–Sun 1400–1600; Gallery Tue–Sun 1130–1700. Shop with modern art

Sedgwick Museum

books and postcards. Disabled access to the gallery from Castle Street but access to the house is limited. ☎ 352124

Scott Polar Research Institute, Lensfield Road. Founded in 1920 as a memorial to Robert Falcon Scott and his four companions who died on their way back from the South Pole in 1912, the institute is the most important polar library and archive in the world. The museum displays relics, important diaries, letters, water colours, drawings, photographs, clothing and travelling equipment from the expeditions of Captain Scott and many other polar explorers. There are displays of native life in the Arctic, Eskimo and Lapp arts and crafts, wildlife, and modern scientific research. Collections not displayed are accessible to members of the public who have a specialised interest.

Admission free. Open Mon–Sat 1430–1600, with the exception of some university and public holidays. Groups by appointment only. Shop. Disabled access. ☎ 336540

Sedgwick Museum of Geology, Downing Street.

Belonging to the Department of Earth Sciences, the museum houses an important collection of fossils. It includes mounted skeletons of fossil mammals and birds, a dinosaur skeleton, marine and flying reptiles, fish, plants and invertebrates from around the world, all arranged by geological age. It also houses Britain's oldest intact geological collection, that of John Woodward (1665–1728), in its original walnut cabinets.

Admission free. Open Mon–Fri 0900–1300 and 1400–1700, Sat 1000–1300. Shop. Disabled access is available on request. ☎ 333456

Whipple Museum of the History of Science, Free School Lane. Founded in 1944 and housed in the seventeenth-century Free School, the museum has a fascinating collection of early scientific instruments from the fourteenth century to the beginning of the twentieth. There are microscopes, telescopes and other astro-nomical instruments, astrolabes, air-pumps, electrical instruments, calculating instru-ments and balances, navigation and survey-ing instruments and sundials. There is a regular programme of special exhibitions.

Admission free. Open Mon–Fri 1330–1630 all year except public holidays. Check for other closures during university vacations. Postcards and literature on sale. Disabled access by arrangement. ☎ 334500 □

The interior of Kettle's Yard –
the first floor of the cottage

Galleries

The Lawson Gallery, King's Parade

In recent years the Cambridge cultural scene has been much enlivened by the appearance of a number of intimate galleries with wide-ranging interests. The major exhibitions to be found at the Fitzwilliam Museum in Trumpington Street and at Kettle's Yard at the lower end of Castle Hill have been touched on in the 'Museums' section but now commercial galleries in various parts of the city are offering the discerning visitor a huge choice of artistic treasures from modern oils and watercolours to antique prints and maps as well as twenty-first-century ceramics and metalwork.

The Art Market, Heffers Art and Graphics Shop, 15–23 King Street. Self-service style art gallery. A thousand original works of art, including paintings, drawings, prints, photo-

Cambridge Contemporary Art

graphs and mixed media by fifty contemporary UK artists. Bespoke framing service. Open Mon–Sat 0900–1700, but Tue 0930–1700. ☎ 568495

Broughton House Gallery, 98 King Street. Regular exhibitions of British and international contemporary art. Open Tue–Sat 1030–1730 or by appointment.
☎ 314960

Cambridge Brass-rubbing Centre, Bridge Street. One hundred facsimiles of the original memorials are available for rubbing. Individuals, families and groups can be catered for. The centre, in the Church of the Holy Sepulchre (Round Church) is open every day: winter 1300–1600; summer 1000–1700 and at other times by appointment. ☎ 871621/ 0831 839261

Cambridge Contemporary Art Galleries, 6 Trinity Street. Leading print publishers; sculptures and other applied arts such as ceramics and textiles. Framing service. Regular changes of exhibitions and occasional demonstrations. Open Mon–Sat 0900–1730. ☎ 324222

Cambridge Darkroom, Dales Brewery, Gwydir Street. Features touring exhibitions of photographs. Includes talks, videos, workshops and discussions. Darkroom

facilities and classes available. Magazines and books for sale. Open Tue–Sun 1200–1700. ☎ 566725

Conservatory Gallery, 6 Hills Avenue. Exhibits include paintings, sculpture and wall-hangings by over fifty of East Anglia's leading artists. Open Sat and the first Sun in each month 1000–1700, and any other time by prior arrangement. ☎ 211311

Fitzwilliam Museum. See under 'Museums'.

Julia Heffer, 1 Sussex Street. Contemporary jewellery, studio glass, ceramics, leather, furniture and textiles. Monthly programme of exhibitions by individual artists. Jewellery made to our own design or to commission. Open Mon–Sat 0930–1730. ☎ 367699

Kettle's Yard. See under 'Museums'.

Lawson Gallery, 7–8 King's Parade. Exhibiting and selling antique prints and maps, modern art posters, Cambridge University prints and posters and art postcards. Framing workshop. Open Mon–Sat 0930–1730 and Sun during summer.
☎ 313970

Primavera, 10 King's Parade. Fine examples of leading British contemporary ceramics, wood, glass, craft work, metal, jewellery and paintings. Open Mon–Sat 0930–1730. ☎ 357708

Regency Gallery, 39 Fitzroy Street. Framing while you wait, prints, limited editions and originals for sale. Restoration and cleaning available. Open Mon–Sat 0900–1700. ☎ 365454

Sebastian Pearson, 3 Pembroke Street (above Peter Crabbe Antiques). British watercolours and oils, mostly from 1840–1940. Also twentieth-century British prints, particularly etchings, drypoints and lithographs from 1900–1940. Two exhibitions annually of selected living artists. Open Mon–Sat 1030–1700. ☎ 323999 □

Eating out

Rutlands Restaurant, University Arms Hotel

The wide variety of cuisines offered by Cambridge restaurants reflects the city's international reputation. Indeed much of the time the atmosphere in many restaurants also has a highly international flavour with foreign tourists, overseas students of English, university 'grads' and dons eating side-by-side with local residents and folk from the countryside who have come into town for a special occasion. There is splendid local produce available to caterers, much of it to be found on the stalls of the city's market, open every day — farm vegetables and fruit, fresh fish caught by Norfolk and Suffolk fishermen and fine cheeses.

English

All Bar One, 36 St Andrew's Street ☎ 371081. Open Mon–Sat 1200–2300, Sun 1200–2230.

Ancient Shepherds, High Street, Fen Ditton ☎ 293280. Open Mon–Sat 1200–1430 and 1830–2130.

Browns, 23 Trumpington Street ☎ 461655. Open Mon–Sat 1100–2330, Sun and Bank hols 1200–2330.

Corner House, 7–9 King Street ☎ 359962. Open Mon–Fri 1130–1430 and 1700–2130, Sat and Sun 1130–2130.

Garfunkels, 21–24 Bridge Street ☎ 311053. Open Mon–Sat 1000–2330, Sun 1000–2230.

Green Man (Beefeater Steak House), 55 High Street, Trumpington ☎ 844903. Bar open Mon–Sat 1100–2300, Sun 1200–2230; restaurant open Mon–Thu 1200–2200, Fri 1200–2230, Sat 1200–2300, Sun 1200–2100.

Loch Fyne (seafood restaurant), 37 Trumpington Street ☎ 362433. Open Mon–Sat 1000–2230, Sun 1000–2130.

No. 1 King's Parade, 1 King's Parade ☎ 359506. Open Mon–Fri 1200–1500, 1800–2230, Sat and Sun 1200–1600, 1800–2230.

Restaurant Twenty-Two, 22 Chesterton Road ☎ 351880. Open Tue–Sat 1900–2130. Open Mon in December only.

The Roof Garden Restaurant (Arts Theatre), Peas Hill ☎ 578930. Open Mon–Sat 1000–2100.

Sticky Fingers, 26 Regent Street ☎ 363088. Open Mon–Fri 1200–1500 and 1800–2230, Sat 1200–1500 and 1700–2230, Sun 1200–2200.

Tatties, 11 Sussex Street ☎ 358478. Open Mon–Fri 0800–2100, Sat 1000–2100.

Travellers' Rest (Beefeater Steak House), Huntingdon Road, Girton ☎ 276182. Bar open Mon–Sat 1100–2300, Sun 1200–2230; restaurant open Mon–Thu 1200–1430 and 1800–2100, Fri 1200–1400 and 1800–2200, Sat 1200–2300, Sun 1200–2100.

University Arms Hotel, Regent Street ☎ 351241. Rutlands Restaurant open for breakfast, lunch and dinner Mon–Fri and Sun; phone for opening times.

Varsity Restaurant (English and Cypriot), 35 St Andrew's Street ☎ 356060. Open every day 1200–1430 and 1730–2245.

'Venue' 66, Regent Street ☎ 367333. Open Mon–Sat 1200–1500 and 1800–2300, Sun 1200–1500 and 1800–2200. Live music.

American

Burger King, 64 St Andrew's Street ☎ 350324. Open every day 1000–2300.

Browns

Chili's, Abbeygate House, 164–167 East Road ☎ 505678. Open Mon–Sat 1130–2300, Sun 1130–2200.

Footlights (Mexican and Texan), Fitzroy Street ☎ 323434. Open every day 1200–2230.

Kentucky Fried Chicken, 174 East Road ☎ 321034. Open Sun–Thu 1100–2400, Fri–Sat 1100–0100.

MacDonalds, Madingley Road ☎ 366753. Open Mon–Sat 0800–2300, Sun 1000–2300.

MacDonalds, Rose Crescent ☎ 303020. Open Sun–Thu 0730–2300, Fri–Sat 0730–2400.

Old Orleans (American Deep South), 10–11 Mill Lane ☎ 322777. Open Mon–Sat 1100–2300, Sun and Bank Holidays 1200–2230.

French

Café Rouge, 24–26 Bridge Street ☎ 364961. Open Mon–Sat 1000–2300, Sun 1000–2230.

The Dome, 33–34 St Andrew's Street ☎ 313818. Open Mon–Sat 0900–2300, Sun 0900–2230.

Galleria, 33 Bridge Street ☎ 362054. Open every day 1200–2300.

Hobbs Pavilion, Parker's Piece ☎ 367480. Open Tue–Sat 1200–1430 (last orders 1415) and 1900–2200 (last orders 2145). Crêperie. Also vegetarian and vegan food.

Michel's Brasserie, 21–24 Northampton Street ☎ 353110. Open every day 1200–1430 and 1800–2300.

Midsummer House, Midsummer Common ☎ 369299. Open Tue–Fri 1200–1400 and 1900–2200, Sun 1200–1400.

Panos, 154 Hills Road ☎ 212958. Open Mon–Fri 1200–1430 and 1900–2200, Sat 1900–2300.

Pierre Victoire, 92 Regent Street ☎ 570170. Open every day 1200–1500 and 1730–2300.

Greek, Cypriot and Turkish

Efes Restaurant (Turkish), 78–80 King Street ☎ 500005. Open Mon–Sat 1200–1400 and 1800–2300, Sun 1200–2300.

Blackboard menu at the Eraina Taverna

Eraina Taverna, 2 Free School Lane ☎ 368786. Open Mon–Fri 1200–1430 and 1730–2330, Sat 1200–2330, Sun 1200–2300.

Panos Restaurant, 154 Hills Road ☎ 212958. Open Mon–Fri 1200–1400 and 1900–2200, Sat 1900–2200.

Varsity Restaurant (Cypriot and English), 35 St Andrew's Street ☎ 356060. Open every day 1200–1430 and 1730–2245.

Indian and Middle Eastern

Bengal, 4 Fitzroy Street ☎ 351010. Open Mon–Sat 1200–1430 and 1800–2400, Sun 1800–2400.

Bodrum, 59 Hills Road ☎ 369696. Open Mon–Fri 1200–1430 and 1800–0200; Sat–Sun 1800–0200.

Cambridge Tandoori, 12B Victoria Avenue ☎ 313331. Open Sun–Thu 1200–1400 and 1800–2400, Fri–Sat 1200–1400 and 1800–2430.

Castle Tandoori, 71 Castle Street ☎ 312569. Open every day 1200–1430 and 1800–2400.

Curry Centre, 45–47 Castle Street ☎ 363666. Open every day 1200–1430 and 1800–2400.

Curry King, 5 Jordan's Yard (off Bridge Street) ☎ 324351. Open every day 1200–1430 and 1800–2400.

Curry Mahal, 3–5 Miller's Yard ☎ 360409. Open every day 1200–1430 and 1800–2400.

Curry Queen, 106 Mill Road ☎ 351027. Open every day 1200–1430 and 1800–2400.

The Gandhi, 72 Regent Street ☎ 353942. Open every day 1200–1430 and 1800–2400.

Golden Curry, 111–113 Mill Road ☎ 329432. Open every day 1200–1430 and 1800–2400.

The Gulshan, 111–113 Mill Road ☎ 353942. Open every day 1200–1430 and 1800–2400.

India House, 31 Newnham Road ☎ 461661. Open every day 1130–1430 and 1800–2400.

Maharajah, 9–13 Castle Street ☎ 358399. Open every day 1200–1430 and 1800–2400.

Meghna Balti House, 36A Mill Road ☎ 576266. Open every day 1200–2400.

Rajbelash Tandoori, 36–38 Hills Road ☎ 354679. Open every day 1200–1430 and 1800–2400.

Shalimar, 84 Regent Street ☎ 355378. Open Mon–Fri 1130–1430 and 1730–2400, Sat and Sun 1130–2400.

Sultans, 17 Hills Road ☎ 354605. Open every day 1200–0300.

Italian

Bella Pasta, The Mill, Newnham Road ☎ 367507. Open every day 1200–2300.

Caffè Piazza, 83 Regent Street ☎ 356666. Open Mon 1000–1500, Tue–Sat 1000–2400. Themed music nights Fri and Sat.

Caffè Uno, 32 Bridge Street ☎ 314954. Open Mon–Sat 1000–2400, Sun 1000–2300.

Don Pasquale, 12A Market Hill ☎ 367063. Open every day 0800–2200.

Don Pasquale Restaurant, 12 Market Hill ☎ 350106. Open Mon–Sat 1200–1500 and 1800–2300.

Mamma Amalfi, 106 Grafton Centre ☎ 462464. Open every day 0900–2230.

La Margherita, 15 Magdalene Street ☎ 315232. Open every day 1200–1430 and 1800–2300.

La Mimosa Bar Ristorante, 4 Rose Crescent ☎ 362525. Open every day 1145–1500, Wed–Sat 1830–2430.

Pizza Express, 28 St Andrew's Street ☎ 361320. Open every day 1130–2400.

Pizza Hut, 66 St Andrew's Street ☎ 323616. Open Sun–Thu 1130–2200, Fri–Sat 1130–2300.

Pizza Hut, 19 Regent Street ☎ 323737. Open Sun–Thu 1200–2300, Fri–Sat 1200–2330.

Trattoria Pasta Fresca, 66 Mill Road ☎ 352836. Open every day 1200–1430 and 1800–2230.

Oriental

Bangkok City (Thai), 24 Green Street ☎ 354382. Open every day 1200–1500 and 1815–2300.

Charlie Chan (Chinese), 14 Regent Street ☎ 361763. Open every day 1200–1415 and Tue–Sun 1800–2330.

Chato Singapore Restaurant, (Singaporian/Malaysian) 2–4 Lensfield Road ☎ 364115. Open Tue–Sat 1200–1400, Mon–Sat 1800–2300.

Chopsticks (Pekinese and Cantonese), 22A Magdalene Street ☎ 566510. Open Tue–Sun 1200–1430 and 1730–2330.

DoJo Noodle Bar (Japanese, Vietnamese and Thai), 1–2 Miller's Yard, Mill Lane ☎ 363471. Open Mon–Thu 1200–1430 and 1730–2300, Fri and Sat 1200–2300.

Hotpot Chinese Restaurant, 66 Chesterton Road ☎ 366552. Open daily 1200–1400 and 1800–2330.

Peking (Pekinese), 21 Burleigh Street ☎ 354755. Open every day 1200–1430 and 1800–2300.

Sala Thong (Thai), 35 Newnham Road ☎ 323178. Open Tue–Sun 1200–1500 and 1800–2300.

Shao Tao (Chinese), 72 Regent Street ☎ 353942. Open Mon–Sat 1200–1430 and 1800–2300.

Tai Cheun (Chinese), 12 St John's Street ☎ 358281. Open daily 1200–1400 and 1800–2230.

Thai Regent, 108 Regent Street ☎ 464355. Open Tue–Sun 1200–1430 and 1800–2300.

Spanish

The Spanish Tapas Bar, The Bun Shop, 1 King Street ☎ 366866. Open Sun–Fri 1800–2400, Sat 1200–2400.

Vegetarian

Most restaurants now offer vegetarian dishes.

Hobbs Pavilion (crêperie with vegetarian and vegan menus), Parker's Piece ☎ 367480. Open Tue–Sat 1200–1415 and 1900–2145.

The Rainbow 9A King's Parade ☎ 321551. Open Mon–Sat 1100–2300.

Cafés and bars

Auntie's Tea Shop, St Mary's Passage ☎ 315641. Open Mon–Fri 0930–1730, Sat 0930–1830, Sun 1200–1730.

Baker's Oven, 68 St Andrew's Street ☎ 355132. Open Mon–Sat 0830–1700.

Bar Coast, The Quayside ☎ 556961. Open Mon–Sat 0930–2300, Sun 0930–2230.

The Bun Shop, 1 King Street ☎ 366866. Open every day. Finnegan's Bar 0930–2300, Wine Bar/Restaurant 1200–2400, Tapas Bar 1200–2400.

Café Carrington, 23 Market Street ☎ 361792. Open Mon–Sat 0800–1700, occasional Sundays.

Café Carrington, Grafton Centre ☎ 460868. Open Mon–Sat 0900–1715, Sun 1030–1630.

Café Thirty-One Bar, Quayside ☎ 312730. Open every day 0930–2230.

CB1 Computer Café, 32 Mill Road ☎ 576306. Open every day 1000–2000.

CB2 Computer Café, 5–7 Norfolk Street ☎ 508503. Open every day 0800–2300.

Clowns Coffee Bar, 54 King Street ☎ 355711. Open every day 0730–2400.

Copper Kettle, 4 King's Parade ☎ 365068. Open Mon–Sat 0830–1730, Sun 0900–1730.

Debenhams, Grafton Centre ☎ 353525. Open Mon–Fri 0900–1730 (Wed until 1930), Sat 0930–1730, Sun 1100–1700.

Delifrance, Market Passage ☎ 721833. Open Mon–Sat 0900–1700, Sun 1000–1700.

Henry's, 5A Pembroke Street ☎ 361206. Open Mon–Sat 0900–1730.

Henry's Café Bar, Quayside ☎ 324649. Open Mon–Sat 0900–2300, Sun 0900–2230.

Indigo Coffee House, 8 St Edward's Passage ☎ 0771 2187839. Open Mon–Sat 1000–2300, Sun 1100–1800.

Internet Exchange Café, 2 St Mary's Passage ☎ 327600. Open Mon–Sat 1000–2000, Sun 1000–1800.

Livingstones, St Andrew's Baptist Church, St Andrew's Street ☎ 566030. Open Mon–Sat 1000–1600.

Martin's Coffee House, 4 Trumpington Street ☎ 361757. Open Mon–Fri 0730–1800, Sat and Sun 0800–1700.

Merrion Coffee Bar (The Fitzwilliam Museum), Trumpington Street ☎ 332900. Open Tue–Sat 1030–1600, Sun 1415–1615.

Savino's, 3 Emmanuel Street ☎ 566186. Open Mon–Fri 0800–1800, Sat 1000–1800.

Steps, 3B Market Hill ☎ 352607. Open Mon–Sat 0800–1730.

Trockel, Ulmann and Freunde, 13 Pembroke Street ☎ 460923. Open Mon–Sat 0900–1645.

Fish and chips

The Fish and Chip Shop, 12 Burleigh Street ☎ 369157. Open 1030–1700. □

Rose Crescent

Pubs

The galleried courtyard of The Eagle pub in Bene't Street

here can be few places where social and class distinctions are so completely erased as in the pubs of Cambridge. Dons, professional people, artisans, students, tourists — all mix happily together. To be lonely in a Cambridge pub is almost an impossibility for here good conversation rates - almost! - as highly as the quality of the beer. Most pubs in the centre are open all day 1100–2300, except on Sundays when opening is normally 1200–2300. Please remember — pub landlords and managers change frequently as do their drink and food serving times, and overseas visitors should note that it is illegal to sell alcohol to people under eighteen.

City centre pubs

The Anchor, Silver Street ☎ 353554
Riverside terrace, split levels inside, punt-hiring station outside. Food is available Mon–Thu 1200–2000, Fri & Sat 1200–1700, Sun 1200–1400.

The Baron of Beef, Bridge Street
☎ 505022. Perhaps the longest bar in Cambridge. Much used by dons and students from St John's College, opposite, and nearby Magdalene College. Bar snacks from 1130.

The Bath, Bene't Street ☎ 358006.
Georgian-fronted medieval inn with large fireplaces. Food is available 1200–1430.

The Bun Shop, King Street ☎ 366866.
A traditional English bar plus restaurants serving English, French and Spanish food. Meals are served all day.

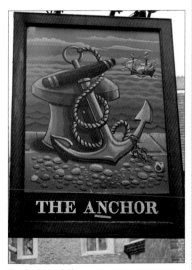

The Anchor pub sign

The Cambridge Rattle and Hum, King Street ☎ 505015. A former brewery, now a comfortable drinking- and eating-house with courtyard seating. Snacks and meals are available from 1200–1630. Children are welcome until 1800. Bar billiards, pool and darts.

The Champion of the Thames, King Street ☎ 352043. Small, cosy, unchanging; beer from the barrel; thirteenth-century building. Food is available at weekdays 1200–1400.

The Eagle, Bene't Street ☎ 505020.
Superbly restored seventeenth-century coaching-inn with galleried courtyard. Its Air Force Bar has names and numbers of war-time Royal Air Force and US squadrons burned on the ceiling with candle smoke. No music or fruit machines. Food is served every day 1200–1430, Mon–Thu 1700–2045 and Fri 1700–2000.

The Granta, Newnham Road ☎ 505016.
Riverside pub with patio overlooking mill pond and Sheep's Green. Refurbished but still traditional interior. Snacks and meals are served Mon–Sat 1200–1400 and 1800–2000, Sun 1200–1400.

The Maypole, Portugal Place ☎ 352999.
Present landlord famed for his cocktails and malt whiskies. Outside courtyard. Food is available for lunch and evenings.

Hogshead, 69–73 Regent Street
☎ 323405. Overlooks Parker's Piece, specialising in real ale and serving twenty different ales at any one time. Guest ales changed every two to three days. Traditional English food available Sun–Thu 1200–2030, Fri–Sat 1200–1900.

The King Street Run, King Street
☎ 328900. Tut and Shive real ale pub, with a minimum of six real·ales at any time

and one guest beer from a micro-brewery. Unusual, lively environment, popular with students at weekends. Satellite TV showing sport. Basket meals are available Mon–Thu 1200–1400, Fri–Sun 1200–1700.

The Mitre Tavern, Bridge Street ☎ 358403. A pub since 1754, now selling several real ales. Food is served Mon–Fri 1130–1430 and 1800–2030, Sat 1200–1600, Sun 1200–1800. Children are welcome if eating.

The Pickerel, Magdalene Street ☎ 355068. The Pickerel claims to be the oldest pub in Cambridge, 600 years old, and almost certainly used by Samuel Pepys when he was a student at Magdalene College across the road. A 'pickerel' is a young pike. There is a patio available for customers in summer. Food is served Sun–Thu 1200–1930, Fri 1200–2100, Sat 1200–1900.

The Red Cow, Wheeler Street ☎ 360021. Situated close to the market square, this is almost an EU pub - it also calls itself *La Vache Rouge* and *Die Rote Kuh*. Breakfast is served from 0830, restaurant 1100–1900. Snacks are available all day. Coffee bar. Food Mon–Thu 1200–2000, Fri–Sun 1200–1600.

Saint Radegund, King Street ☎ 311794. Small, triangular bar. A traditional beer-and-sandwiches pub.

The Rat and Parrot, Downing Street ☎ 304357. Large, modern pub in a famously named street. Food is available all day from 1100.

The Rat and Parrot (formerly The Spade and Becket), Thompson's Lane ☎ 311701. Occupies a fine position overlooking the river and Jesus Green. Large conservatory and seating on the riverside. Food is available all day every day, including Sun.

The Regal, St Andrew's Street ☎ 366459. Part of the J.D. Wetherspoon group, this former cinema claims to be the largest pub in Britain. There is a good range of real ales. Food Mon–Fri 1100–2200, Sat 1200–2200.

The Tap and Spile (The Mill), Mill Lane ☎ 357026. Overlooking the Mill Pond and close to two punt-hiring stations, most of this pub's beer in summer is drunk outside on the bridge or on Laundress Green. Food is served at lunchtime.

The Town and Gown, Pound Hill ☎ 353791. The building is around 400 years old. Food is available every lunchtime Mon–Thu 1830–2200.

And a few little further out ...

The Boathouse, Chesterton Road ☎ 460905. Popular riverside pub overlooking Jesus Green. Occasional comedy. Food is available Mon–Fri 1200–1500, Mon–Thu 1800–2100, Sat 1200–1500, Sun 1200–1800. Children are welcome until 2100.

The Cambridge Blue, Gwydir Street, ☎ 361382. Cosy Victorian pub. Food is available Mon–Sat 1200–1400 and 1800–2130

The Castle, St Andrew's Street ☎ 506200. Used by students from Emmanuel College across the road and locals. Food is available at lunchtime only.

The Castle Inn, Castle Street, ☎ 353194. Close to Castle Mound, this pub is popular with students. Not open all day. Food is available Mon–Sat 1800–2130, Sun 1200–1430 and 1900–2130.

The Clarendon Arms, Clarendon Street, ☎ 313937. Terrace pub. Food is available Mon–Sat 1200–1430 and 1830–2100, Sun 1200–1430.

The Cricketers, Melbourne Place ☎ 516701. Garden. Children are welcome. Half-price student meals are available, and food is served every day 1200–1430, Tue–Sat 1900–2100.

The Elm Tree, Orchard Street ☎ 633005. Small but comfortable. Snacks and meals are served every day 1200–1500, Tue–Sun 1800–2100.

The Fort St George, Midsummer Common, ☎ 354327. Popular 400-year-old riverside pub overlooking college boathouses. Children are welcome in the garden. Open all day in summer. Food is served every day, in summer 1200–1430 and 1730–2100; in winter 1200–1430 and 1900–2100.

The Fountain, Regent Street ☎ 366540. This pub has a large, mock Victorian bar. Children are welcome at lunchtime. Food is available Mon–Sat 1100–1900, Sun 1200–1900.

The Free Press, 5–7 Prospect Row (behind the Police Station) ☎ 368337. This pub has real ale and a real fire. Traditional atmosphere – no smoking, gaming or mobile phones. Food daily 1200–1400 and 1800–2100.

The Fresher and Firkin, Chesterton Road ☎ 324325. There are two bars, and up-stairs is available for private functions. There is satellite TV, and live music is played on weekend evenings. There is also a micro-brewery on site, providing in-house ales. Food is available daily 1200–1500 and 1800–2100.

The Prince Regent, Regent Street ☎ 505030. This is a former coaching-inn, which backs onto Parker's Piece. Food is available Mon–Sat 1200–1400 and 1800–2000, Sun 1200–1400.

Sir Isaac Newton, Castle Street ☎ 505018. Well-designed pub with much Newtonia in evidence. Food is available Mon–Sat 1200–1400 and 1800–2000, Sun 1200–1400.

Tram Depot, 5 Dover Street ☎ 324553. This pub is on the site of stables that were used by the old tram horses. It serves traditional beers, and authentic Czech Budweiser is on tap. There is a no-smoking area. Children are welcome. All the food is home-cooked, Egon Ronay recommended. It is available daily 1200–1400, Mon–Fri 1800–2100.

Pubs with Music
See under Entertainment, p. 141.

Bars
Modern bars are now very much a part of the Cambridge scene. All of them serve interesting food and drink.
They include:

All Bar One, St Andrew's Street ☎ 371081

Bar Coast, Quayside ☎ 556961

Ha Ha Bar, Trinity Street ☎ 305089

Henry's Bar, Quayside ☎ 324649

Lawyers Wine and Oyster Bar, Lensfield Road ☎ 566887   ☐

Shopping

Crabtree &
Evelyn in
Market Street

Because of its triple role as county town, university city and international tourist attraction, Cambridge has developed a widely varied mix of shopping facilities, ranging from large department stores to small, specialist outlets and, as you might think, it has some of the country's best new, second-hand and anti-quarian bookshops.

The city has two shopping centres: one based on the old, traditional market-place and the other at the new Grafton Centre. The city centre is closed to motor traffic between 1000 and 1600 from Monday to Saturday, which makes it a pleasant and safe shopping environment. But do beware the many bicycles ...

Most shops are open between 0900 and 1730 Monday to Saturday but some large stores stay open later on Wednesday evening. Some shops now also open on Sunday especially during the main tourist season.

The **open-air market** has been the centre of Cambridge life for over 800 years, and its stalls offer a remarkable number of different goods: fresh fruit and local vegetables, fresh fish from the east coast, including lobster and Cromer crabs, fine cheeses, second-hand books, sheepskin products, hats, small antiques, ethnic goods, new and second-hand clothes, flowers, plants, jewellery, paintings and souvenirs and Cambridge T-shirts.

Around the **market square** are banks, specialist clothes and shoe shops, jewellers, Paperchase and one of the two Marks & Spencer shops in the city. This one has a food hall, men's wear and home furnishings.

A number of shopping streets radiate from the market. In the south-east corner is pedestrianised **Petty Cury** with modern fashion shops, jewellers, a Disney Store and an entrance to the **Lion Yard**, Cambridge's first covered shopping precinct, opened by Princess Anne in the 1960s, with a large variety of shops, including HMV Music Shop, The Body Shop, an Early Learning Centre, fashion shops and Culpeper's, the herbalists. The Central Library is here. The extended and refurbished Lion Yard is designed to provide more shopping space.

Market Street, one of the oldest shopping streets in the city, runs from the north-east corner of the market. It has a betting shop, Crabtree & Evelyn toiletries, Wax Lyrical candles, a coffee bar, boutiques, W.H. Smith's and mobile telephone shops.

Pedestrianised **Rose Crescent** leads off the north side of the market-place. It has a number of exclusive shops for fashion, leather, crystal and china, a well-disguised MacDonalds, Cellini, the pearl specialist, and Lingard's game and jigsaw shop.

North-west of the market is **Trinity Street**, one of the most attractive streets in Cambridge with its exceptionally fine façades. On the corner, the Cambridge University Press bookshop, where books have been sold since 1581. The street also has Heffer's main and children's bookshops and Heffers Sound, as well as exclusive men's and women's fashion shops, a sports equipment shop, an antique jewellers and an art gallery.

St Mary's Passage, leading from the Market to **King's Parade** has Internet Exchange, an internet café. King's Parade is the city's best-known thoroughfare, with university outfitters, galleries, fine clothes

Heffer's Children's Bookshop

shops, an ecclesiastical bookshop, a camera equipment shop, a National Trust shop and a teddy-bear shop.

Confusingly, Cambridge's main street, which follows the line of the old Roman road, has seven different names. At the south end, **Regent Street** has good antique shops with more round the corner in **Lensfield Road**. Moving back towards the city centre, **St Andrew's Street** has Robert Sayles, a John Lewis department store, and further along, now in **Sidney Street**, the main entrance to Boots, the chemists, and the second Marks & Spencer's, selling ladies' fashions, lingerie and children's wear, and the American Express Travel Bureau. Sidney Street also has excellent bookshops and Sainsbury's, the only supermarket outlet in the city centre. **Green Street**, on the left, has Past Times, designer clothes shops and ethnic shops. Continuing into **Bridge Street** – we are still on the old Roman road – there are fashion shops and gift shops and a number of restaurants. On the **Quayside**, beside the river, is Hemsleys Needlecrafts Specialists. Over the river in **Magdalene Street** is a ladies' hat shop, delicatessens, a silver-smith and other small shops.

King Street, well known for its pubs, has two specialist shops selling new CDs and second-hand records, a coffee shop and cafés. Heffers art and graphics shop and designer fashion shops.

Cambridge's newest shopping centre, the **Grafton Centre**, is a short walk from the Drummer Street bus station across New Square. The Centre has its own car parks with 1,300 spaces and is a drop off point for all local bus routes and the park and ride services. There are more than seventy shops from small specialists to large national stores, including Debenhams, C&A and Bhs. There is a 350-seat food court, two cafés, two fast-food outlets, three restaurants and an eight-screen Warner Brothers Multiplex. The Centre is open seven days a week, Sundays from 1100-1700 with late-night shopping on Wednesdays. They operate a Shop-mobility scheme.

Shop-mobility scheme

See the section 'Getting Around'.

Crafts and collectables

All Saints' Gardens, Trinity Street; opposite main entrance to St John's College. Open-air craft market on summer weekends 1000–1700 and Christmas and Easter. Local artists selling pottery, paintings, jewellery and clothes.

Market Square. On Sundays from 1030 to 1630 there is an art, craft and antiques market in the centre of Cambridge. There is also an organic market where farmers, market gardeners and butchers sell their own produce.

Fisher Hall, Guildhall Street. Craft fair selling books, antiques and clothing on selected Sat 1000–1700, also occasionally during the week.

Banks

Abbey National, 60–61 St Andrew's Street. Open Mon, Tue, Thu and Fri 0900–1700, Wed 0930–1700, Sat 0900–1600. ☎ 350495

Alliance & Leicester, 36 Fitzroy Street. Open Mon, Tue, Wed and Fri 0900–1700; Thu 1000–1700, Sat 0900–1200. ☎ 355473

Alliance & Leicester, 49 Sidney Street. Open Mon, Tue, Thu and Fri 0900–1700, Wed 1000–1700, Sat 0900–1600. ☎ 362362

Barclays Bank, 30 Market Hill. Open Mon, Tue, Thu and Fri 0900–1700, Wed 1000–1700, Sat 0930–1500. ☎ 542000

Barclays Bank, 15 Bene't Street. Open Mon, Tue, Thu and Fri 0900–1700, Wed 1000–1700. ☎ 542000

Barclays Bank, 35 Sidney Street. Open Mon, Tue, Thu and Fri 0900–1700, Wed 1000–1700. ☎ 542000

Bradford & Bingley, 9 Trinity Street. Open Mon–Fri 0900–1700, Sat 0900–1200. ☎ 359745

Cheltenham & Gloucester, 4–5 Peas Hill. Open Mon, Tue, Thu and Fri 0900–1700, Wed 0930–1700, Sat 0900–1200. ☎ 366233

HFC Bank, 75 Regent Street. Open Mon–Sat 0900–1730. ☎ 314822

HSBC Bank, 62 Hills Road. Open Mon–Fri 0930–1700. ☎ 546800

HSBC Bank, 32 Market Hill. Open Mon–Fri 0900–1700, Sat 0930–1530. ☎ 546800

HSBC Bank, 52 St Andrew's Street. Open Mon, Tue, Thu and Fri 0930–1700, Wed 1000–1700. ☎ 546800

Lloyds TSB Bank, 95–97 Regent Street. Open Mon–Fri 0900–1700. ☎ 0845 3030105

Lloyds TSB Bank, 6 St Andrew's Street. Open Mon, Tue, Thu, Fri 0900–1700, Wed 1000–1800. ☎ 460646

Lloyds TSB Bank, 3 Sidney Street. Open Mon–Fri 0900–1700; Sat 1000–1300. ☎ 0845 3030105

Halifax, 30A Fitzroy Street. Open Mon–Fri 0900–1700, Sat 0900–1330. ☎ 0845 6033610

Halifax, 32–33 Petty Cury. Open Mon–Fri 0900–1700, Sat 0900–1600, Sun 1100–1500. ☎ 0845 6033610

National Westminster Bank, 10 Bene't Street. Open Mon–Fri 0900–1630. ☎ 0845 601 3366

National Westminster Bank, 56 St Andrew's Street. Open Mon–Fri 0900–1700, Wed opens at 0930, Sat 0930–1530. ☎ 0845 601 3366

National Westminster Bank, 26 Trinity Street. Open Mon–Fri 0900–1630. ☎ 0845 601 3366

Northern Rock, 26–27 Sidney Street. Open Mon–Fri 0900–1700, Sat 0900–1200. ☎ 367638

Royal Bank of Scotland, 28 Trinity Street. Open Mon–Fri 0915–1645 ☎ 464424

Yorkshire Bank, 6 Jesus Lane. Open Mon, Tue, Thu and Fri 0915–1600, Wed 0945–1800. ☎ 312929

Antiques on sale in Trumpington Street

Woolwich, 57 St Andrew's Street, Open Mon, Tue, Wed, Fri 1900–1700, Thu 0930–1700, Sat 0900–1200. ☎ 359191

Building societies

Britannia, 23–24 Sidney Street. Open Mon–Fri 0900–1700, Sat 0900–1200. ☎ 312066

Cambridge Building Society, 32 St Andrew's Street. Open Mon–Fri 0900–1700, Sat 0900–1600. ☎ 727600

Cambridge Building Society, 73 Bridge Street. Open Mon–Fri 0900–1700, Sat 0900–1200. ☎ 727868

Cambridge Building Society, Grafton Centre. Open Mon–Fri 0900–1700, Sat 0900–1730, Sun 1100–1700. ☎ 727651

Nationwide, 67 St Andrew's Street. Open Mon, Wed–Fri 0900–1700, Tue 0930–1700, Sat 0900–1200. ☎ 542600

Norwich & Peterborough, 27 St Andrew's Street. Open Mon, Wed, Thu and Fri 0900-1700, Tue 0930-1700, Sat 0900-1200. ☎ 303133

Bureaux de change

American Express, 25–27 Sidney Street.
☎ 351636. Lost or stolen cards ☎ 020 7222 9633

Thomas Cook Travel, HSBC Bank, 32 Market Hill
☎ 464147

Thomas Cook Travel, 8 St Andrew's St ☎ 543100

Main post offices

9–11 St Andrew's Street ☎ 323325
23–24 Trinity Street ☎ 352081
33 Regent Street ☎ 352998
29 Hills Road ☎ 354823
2A Trumpington Street ☎ 359596

Main supermarkets

J. Sainsbury, 44 Sidney Street ☎ 366891
J. Sainsbury, Brooks Road ☎ 246183
Tesco Stores, Cambridge Road, Milton ☎ 420178
Tesco Stores, Yarrow Road, Fulbourn ☎ 548300

Cambridge Colleges

This handy guide, published by Jarrold, includes fascinating historical background on each college, along with details of architecture and famous past students. Illustrated throughout with fine colour photography, *Cambridge Colleges* is an ideal way to find out more about the city's world-famous academic community.

CAMBRIDGE COLLEGES

JARROLD

Available locally from Cambridge Tourist Information Centre and all good bookshops

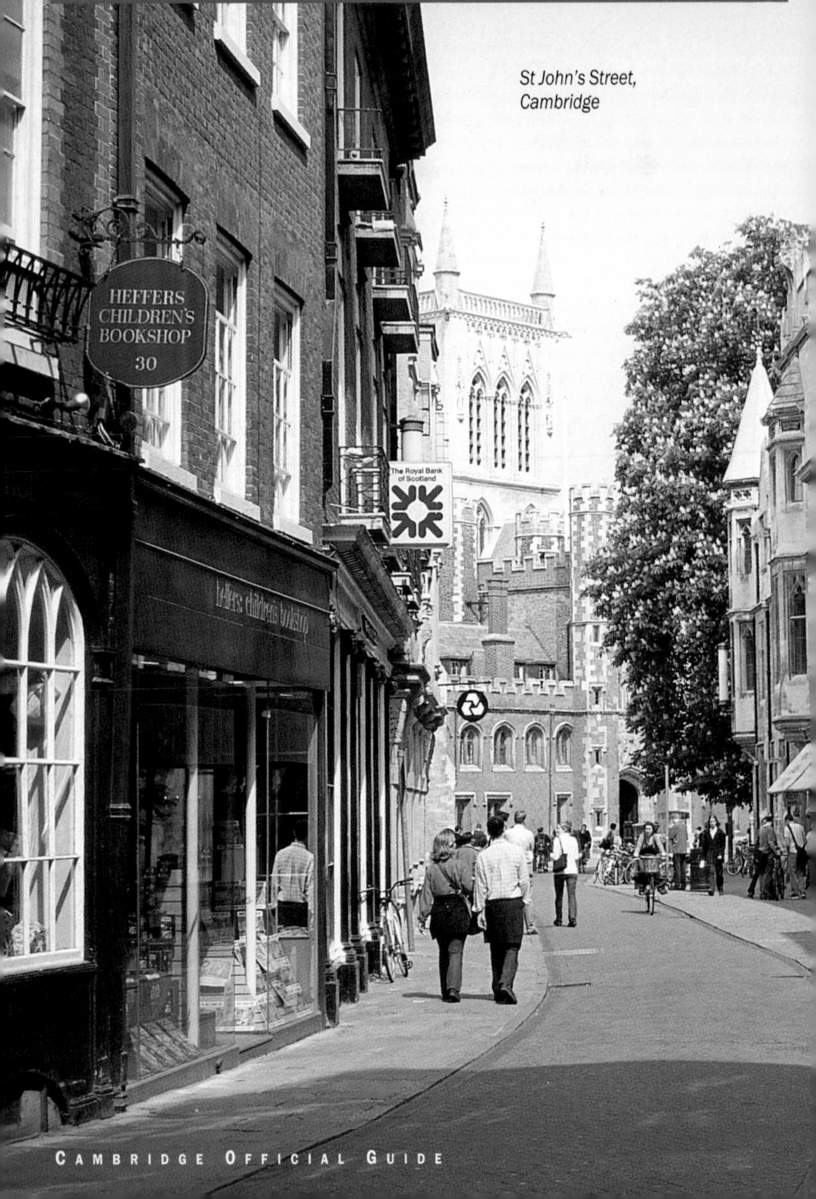

St John's Street,
Cambridge

HEFFERS
CHILDREN'S
BOOKSHOP
30

The Royal Bank
of Scotland

HA!
HA!
Bar &
Canteen
at the·
Blue Boar

JAEGER

Entertainment

Street theatre in the Market Square

Cambridge has a wide range of arts and entertainment events throughout the year. Each summer the City Council Leisure Services bring together most events taking place in the city under the title 'Summer in the City' for which brochures are published at the end of May. Copies are available from the Tourist Information Centre.

The annual Cambridge Folk Festival, held at the end of July, is acknowledged to be one of the world's most important festivals for folk, roots, blues and country music. Classical music concerts and organ recitals can be enjoyed in most college chapels at various times during the year and at the West Road Concert Hall. Also, the various college and university drama societies produce a great assortment of plays and entertainments. The Footlights Revue takes place every year during 'May Week' – in June!

Fairs and circuses are held on Midsummer Common. Midsummer Fair in June is traditionally opened by the Mayor who then throws pennies to children in the crowd. Strawberry Fair, organised by local people, takes place on the first Saturday in June.

There are huge free firework displays in July on Parker's Piece and on Bonfire Night – 5 November – on Midsummer Common.

Rag Week in February brings much gaiety to the city with a parade of decorated floats and students in fancy dress collecting money for various charities. There are numerous 'happenings' – they see who can 'fly' the furthest from Silver Street Bridge before falling into the river, and there is a Bed Race, when students charge round the streets pushing home-made beds bearing apprehensive 'patients'.

Arts centre

The Junction, The Cattle Market, off Clifton Road. Cambridge's first music and arts centre, it is ideal for young people. Programmes include rock bands, jazz, late night clubs, cabaret, theatre and other performing arts. There is a licensed bar and café. ☎ 511511

Cinemas

Cambridge Arts Picturehouse, 38 St Andrew's Street. New films, foreign-language films and late-night shows. Children's matinees most Saturday mornings. ☎ 504444

Warner Brothers Multiscreen Cinema, The Grafton Centre. Eight-screen cinema showing nationwide general releases and late-night shows. Children's matinees most Saturday mornings. Booking advisable. Recorded info. ☎ 460442; Credit card bookings ☎ 460441

Concert halls

The Corn Exchange, Wheeler Street. A Victorian building which has been transformed into a major concert venue — hosts top rock and pop bands as well as full-scale orchestras, comedy, ballet, opera and touring theatre. Box office ☎ 357851

The University Concert Hall, West Road ☎ 335102. This is the concert hall in the University of Cambridge Faculty of Music where you can hear a broad spectrum of classical music. Town and gown musical groups perform here as do many of the college music societies. Tickets from the Arts Theatre Box Office ☎ 503333 or the Corn Exchange, Wheeler Street ☎ 357851

Folk festival

The Charles Wells Cambridge Folk Festival takes place every year at the end of July at Cherry Hinton Hall to the south of the city. For information and to join the free mailing list ☎ Leisure Services Marketing, 457521

Nightlife

Cambridge has a variety of nightclubs, catering for different tastes and age-groups, and a number of pubs that feature live music.

Chicago's, 22 Sidney Street ☎ 324600

Fifth Avenue, Heidelberg Gardens ☎ 362444

The Junction, Clifton Road. Bands, club nights, touring theatre, late-night discos and cabaret. ☎ 511511

Kambar, Wheeler Street ☎ 357503

Po Na Na, 7 Jesus Lane ☎ 323880

Q Club, 1–3 Station Road ☎ 315466

Billy Bragg giving a concert in Cambridge

Corn Exchange

Pubs and Restaurants with music

The Boat Race, 170 East Road. Varied programme of music every night of the week, well-known bands. Comedy night once a month. ☎ 508533

Café Piazza, 83 Regent Street. Pizza restaurant with music. Fri and Sat Latin American nights. ☎ 356666

Devonshire Arms, 1 Devonshire Road. Music 2000–2330 most nights: reggae, calypso, soul, funk, jazz. Club Africa 1st and 3rd Tue each month; salsa, Latin American 2nd and 4th Tue. ☎ 316610

The Elm Tree, Orchard Street. Jazz on Mon, Thu and Sun evenings. ☎ 363005

The Haymakers, 54 High Street, Chesterton. Quiz night Mon and Wed; live music, rock/blues Fri and Sat. ☎ 367417

The Junction, Clifton Road. Live music, comedy, theatre, dance most weekday evenings. Weekends are club nights. ☎ 511511

La Mimosa, 4 Rose Crescent. Continental bar and restaurant with live music to include jazz and Latin American dancing. ☎ 362525

Portland Arms, Mitcham's Corner, Chesterton Rd. Live music Mon–Sat; jazz alt. Sun. ☎ 357268

Quinn's, Downing Street. Traditional Irish music Tue and Thu. ☎ 556500

The Rattle and Hum, King Street. Either a live band or DJ every evening. ☎ 505015

The Rock, 200 Cherry Hinton Road. Live music, rock/blues, at weekends. ☎ 249292

'Venue' 66, Regent Street. Live music: jazz, soul, classical piano. ☎ 367333

The Wrestlers, 337 Newmarket Road. Pub which does Thai food and has live music at weekends, mainly rock and blues. ☎ 566553

Theatres

ADC Theatre, Park Street ☎ 359547 (admin.). Headquarters of the University Dramatic Club but also used by other amateur and professional companies. Fringe theatre in summer. Booking through the Arts Theatre Box Office ☎ 503333

Arts Theatre, Peas Hill. Hosts professional companies: dance, drama, opera, music and comedy, from ground-breaking international productions to traditional pantomime. Bars and restaurants. Full disabled access. ☎ 503333

Cambridge Drama Centre, Covent Garden, off Mill Road. Venue for new theatre, daily community classes and weekend workshops. ☎ 322748

Corn Exchange, Wheeler Street. Victorian building which has been transformed into a major concert venue and theatre – hosts top orchestras and bands as well as comedy, ballet, opera and touring theatre. Box office ☎ 357851

The Junction, Clifton Road. Contemporary theatre, dance and touring groups. ☎ 511511

Mumford Theatre, Anglia Polytechnic University, Broad Street, off East Road. The theatre has a varied programme of theatre, music, dance and opera presented by student, amateur and professional companies. ☎ 352932 ☐

Gardens and open spaces

Spring crocuses at Trinity College

The rights of the ancient commons and open spaces which are 'the lungs' of the City of Cambridge are guarded jealously by its citizens, and any proposals for change are vigorously challenged. The gardens of the colleges are among the most splendid in the United Kingdom, and the University Botanic Garden is internationally renowned. In addition, of course, there are the Backs, unforgettable and loved the world over.

Everywhere around the city centre are open spaces: Midsummer Common, Jesus Green, Parker's Piece, Coe Fen, Christ's Pieces and the spacious grounds of Christ's, Jesus, Emmanuel, Downing and Sidney Sussex colleges.

The Backs

The Backs have developed gradually since the sixteenth century, when the riverside colleges began to reclaim land along the banks of the Cam. Now the visitor sees a combination of tussocky meadow with grazing cattle, weeping willows over-hanging the river and immaculate lawns, gardens and carpets of spring flowers. Beautiful bridges – among them Clare Bridge with its spheres and balusters and the Bridge of Sighs at St John's – span the Cam, linking the colleges and the Backs. There are incomparable views of the west end of King's College Chapel and the Gibbs Building, palatial Clare College and the 'wedding-cake' prospect of the New Court of St John's. No wonder the Backs are said to be among the world's loveliest mixtures of river, lawns, gardens, rare trees and ancient architecture – and no wonder Cambridge has been described as a garden city without rival.

Botanic Garden

The University Botanic Garden, Bateman Street. Widely regarded as second in importance only to Kew Gardens, the Botanic covers more than 40 acres *16 ha*, although part of the grounds are kept for private research. Founded in 1760 on a site off Pembroke Street to discover the virtues of plants 'for the benefit of mankind', the garden was moved to its present position in 1847, and its original role continues unchanged. It is a masterpiece, designed to fascinate professional and amateur botanists alike, famed especially for its systematic beds, each containing a single natural order, and its chronological beds, showing the introduction of plants to Britain). Its winter gardens are as bright as summer equivalents, glasshouses contain the exotic and the bizarre and there is even a display of carnivorous plants. 'The Botanic' holds nine national collections. Open seven days a week, spring 1000–1700, summer 1000–1800, winter 1000–1600 (dates vary).

Admission charge all year daily Mar–Sept. Wed morning 1000–1200 admission free. Guided tours, by prior arrangement, are given by the Friends of the Botanic. ☎ 336265

Botanic Garden

King's College Bridge from the Backs

College gardens

Like the Botanic, many college gardens are magnificent. Although private and normally reserved for the college Fellows, some are open to the public regularly and others on special occasions. Potential visitors to the gardens should check availability with the Tourist Information Centre beforehand.

The 'grander' gardens include those of **Christ's College**, normally open to the public Mon–Fri 1000–1200 and 1400–1600, wherein can be found, amongst its splendours and winding paths, Milton's Mulberry Tree, a row of beehives for the Fellows' honey and a swimming-pool, formerly a 'cold bath', one of many introduced to Cambridge in the seventeenth and eighteenth centuries. **Clare College** Fellows' garden is normally open 1130-1630 during College charging period from Easter to end of Sept, weather permitting. Designed this century by Neville Willmer it has one of the finest of herbaceous borders and a charming sunken garden.

Emmanuel College, with its carp-filled fish-pond, little changed from that of the Dominican monastery on this site before the college's foundation in 1584, is reckoned to have one of the best college gardens. Its trees are spectacular — from the steps of the library can be seen a quarter-mile semicircle of free-standing trees, including the magnificent oriental plane (Platanus orientalis), said to be one of the treasures of England.

Around every corner of even the least-gardened of colleges is a fragrant surprise. In **Trinity Hall**, the beautiful, deep herbaceous border by the sixteenth-century library is overlooked by an almost overpowering Magnolia grandiflora, and in **St John's College**'s 'natural' wilderness garden are beds of martagon lilies (Lilium martagon), envied the world over. The Deer Park in **Peterhouse** — the deer died out in the 1930s — has one of the best displays of daffodils in Cambridge, and there are many yew trees in the grounds of this, Cambridge's oldest college. The Fellows' Garden at **Magdalene College**, usually open to visitors Mon–Sat 1330–1830, has a pets' cemetery, whilst in the Fellows' Garden at **King's College**, sometimes open under the National Gardens Scheme, is a ninety-year-old pride of India or golden-rain tree (Koelreuteria paniculata), the finest example in Cambridge. Such examples are endless.

Visitors must remember that the colleges are private institutions and are therefore able to amend their opening hours according to their individual requirements.

Open spaces

Cherry Hinton Hall

Cherry Hinton Hall (1834) and its 28 acres

11.5 ha of parkland is owned by Cambridge City Council. It has many unusual and rare trees. There is a lake with wildfowl, a toddlers' play-area that includes play equipment for disabled children and paddling-pools. There are several outstanding pieces of modern sculpture in the grounds. The annual Charles Wells Cambridge Folk Festival is held here.

Christ's Pieces

Bought by the Council from Jesus College for an undisclosed sum in 1886, the Pieces cover 10 acres *4 ha* close to the heart of the city. Here, beyond the bowling-green, formal beds containing 17,000 spring and summer bedding-plants and bulbs provide wonderful splashes of colour all year round. There are also hard tennis-courts and a children's play-area. The bowling-green rosebed was planted in honour of the Samaritans 40th anniversary, using the new 'Samaritan' rose variety. In 1999 a rose garden was created in memory of Diana, Princess of Wales.

Coe Fen, Sheep's Green and Lammas Land

All three are adjacent to the River Cam running between Coe Fen and Sheep's Green and are lined with pollard willows. Much of Coe Fen is grazed by cattle and horses, Sheep's Green has a learner swimming-pool open in summer and Lammas Land is given over to recreational facilities with hard tennis-courts, a bowling-green, a play-area and a paddling-pool.

Coldham's Common

Largest of the commons with more than 60 acres *24 ha* of ground, Coldham's Common was once the site of wooden 'pest houses', used to accommodate people afflicted by the plague. In the late nineteenth century it became a rich digging-ground for the fertiliser ingredient known as coprolite — nodules of fossil dung. Fossil-diggers earned £4 a week, compared with 10 shillings (50p) for agricultural workers. Today the common has the biggest area of playing-fields in Cambridge with 35 acres *16 ha* of recreation grounds, including eight football pitches, one American football pitch, and one sporting synthetic pitch at the Abbey Sports Centre. There are two children's play-areas on the Common, which is also grazed by cattle and contains a diversity of wild flora.

Jesus Green

Separated from Midsummer Common by Victoria Avenue, the green saw the burning at the stake of Thomas Thorley, Bishop of

Christ's Pieces

Laundress Green

Norwich in 1554 and later John Hullier, Vicar of Babraham, on Maundy Thursday, 1556. Now the green is a peaceful riverside oasis with fine gardens, tree-lined avenues, an open-air swimming-pool, bowling-green, hard and lawn tennis-courts and a children's play-area. Rounders is popular on summer evenings.

Laundress Green
Here, on an island in the middle of the Cam, is the smallest of the commons. It was once used by washerwomen to dry their clothes, newly washed in the river. Grazed by cattle in the summer, it is also a favourite spot for fishermen, students and visitors who eat and drink there on warm days.

Midsummer Common and Butts Green
Mentioned in the 'Domesday Book' (1086), King John granted a fair here in 1211, and it is still held in June each year, the Mayor proclaiming it at noon on the opening day, before joining in the festivities together with city councillors and officials. Traditionally pennies are thrown to children in the crowd. In the eighteenth century it was called 'Pot Fair' because merchants from far and wide came to auction their china wares. Today it is the site for other fairs, circuses and firework displays. Butts Green is part of the common and, as its name suggests, was once used for archery practice. Grazing by cattle has recently been reintroduced.

The **Fen Rivers Way** begins on Midsummer Common. This is a river walk from Cambridge to Ely.

Parker's Piece
Perhaps the best-known but by no means the oldest open space in Cambridge, Parker's Piece is an almost sacred area of turf for cricketers because here was the

nursery where Cambridge-born Jack Hobbs learned his craft. Today there are still three cricket squares on the Piece, used by local teams. The town acquired it in 1613 in exchange for ground behind Trinity College. The exchange was important topographically because the land obtained by Trinity on both sides of the river, coupled with that acquired by St John's three years earlier, completed that area of land now known as the Backs. The Piece is named after Edward Parker, a Trinity College cook, who farmed it under lease at the time of the transaction. To celebrate Queen Victoria's coronation in 1838, 15,000 people sat at sixty tables on the Piece and ate 1,608 plum puddings! Hobbs Pavilion, opened in 1930 in honour of Sir Jack Hobbs, is now a restaurant.

Queens' Green

Really the beginning of the Backs, the green behind Queens' College is very much a picnicking-area for visitors.

Stourbridge Common

King John also granted a fair here for the Leper Hospital of St Mary Magdalene (see 'Churches' section), and it was to make the name of Cambridge famous throughout Europe. The fair gradually extended to more than three weeks during late autumn and, because the common was bounded by the river along its length, large vessels carrying merchants and their goods from all over the continent could sail upstream to the very heart of the fair. It was so important that it was proclaimed by both Cambridge University and Corporation, and both bodies indulged in much feasting and drinking. For long, a special officer was appointed as ale-taster at the fair — he was called Lord of the Taps. It is not known how old the office was but in 1655 it is recorded that Cambridge Corporation gave money to buy a coat for Michael Wolfe 'he being Lord of the Taps this present yeare'. Gradually the fair declined until it was proclaimed for the last time in 1933 and ended by royal decree. It is thought that Isaac Newton bought his famous prism at the fair and that it served as the model for John Bunyan's 'Vanity Fair'. Today the common has splendid riverside trees and is grazed from April to October. □

The commons and towpaths alongside the river provide plenty of opportunities for casual or longer strolls and walks. The Tourist Information Centre has explanatory leaflets.

Sports

Sport, for both spectator and participant, is abundant in Cambridge and its surrounds, with the local Football League team Cambridge United, university cricket and rugby teams, which all attract opponents of international standard, and with rowing clubs, which have produced Olympic oarsmen, and tiddly-winks, which has received royal patronage.

Nearby to the east is Newmarket, headquarters of British horse-racing with its two racecourses and to the west, Huntingdon, the National Hunt racecourse. In Cambridge, the standard of indoor sporting facilities is particularly high.

Throughout the year there is considerable sporting activity along the River Cam involving boats from city, college and school clubs. Eights, fours, pairs and single sculls are constantly practising on the river north of Midsummer Common. University 'bumping' races take place in February and June and city 'Bumps' in July.

For information on **City Council sports facilities** contact: Sports Development Team, The Guildhall, Cambridge CB2 3QJ ☎ 457534

Public tennis-courts and bowling-greens: bookings and information ☎ 316142/213352

Sports centres

The Abbey Swimming-Pool, Whitehill Road, provides a booking service for City of Cambridge leisure facilities, including cricket, tennis, football, rugby, American football, hockey, netball, the Reflections Gym and the soft play area.
☎ 213352

Cambridge Parkside Pools, Gonville Place. The city's latest state-of-the-art, Lottery-funded swimming-pool providing swimming, diving and flumes. Executive-style health suite, meeting-room facilities, cafeteria. ☎ 446100 (recorded information), 446104 (reception)

Kelsey Kerridge Sports Hall, Queen Anne Terrace. The main indoor sports hall in the area. Facilities for weight training, fitness, badminton, football, volleyball, basketball, hockey, cricket, short tennis, squash, wall-climbing; bar.
☎ 462226

Sports club for the physically handicapped – contact Red Cross Society Office, 2 Shaftesbury Road, Cambridge ☎ 354434

Village Centre, Colville Road, Cherry Hinton. Facilities for badminton, football and volleyball; meeting-rooms available. ☎ 576412

Sports clubs

Angling
A fishing sheet is available from the East of England Tourist Board, Toppesfield Hall, Hadleigh, Suffolk ☎ (01473) 822922, on fresh water and sea fishing. Anglers must have a National Rod Licence, obtainable from all post offices. Thereafter fishing in the River Cam in Cambridge is free. Fishing rights on other stretches belong to different fishing clubs. Permits for these stretches can be bought on the riverbank.
Cambridgeshire and Isle of Ely Federation of Anglers ☎ 861748
Grafham Water (trout fishing), Cambridgeshire ☎ (01480) 810531

Archery
Cambridge City Indoor Bowmen
City of Cambridge Bowmen
For details contact the Sports Development Team ☎ 457534

Athletics
Cambridge and Coleridge Club
For details contact the Sports Development Team ☎ 457534

Badminton
Cherry Hinton Road club
Chesterton club
For details contact the Sports Development Team ☎ 457534

Basketball
Cambridgeshire Basketball Association
☎ (01480) 390935

Bowls
Cambridgeshire and County Bowling Club, Brooklands Avenue ☎ 353615
Also **bowling-greens** at Jesus Green, Christ's Pieces, Alexandra Gardens, Barnwell and Coleridge recreation grounds and Nightingale Avenue.

Cambridgeshire Moat House Hotel golf course

Cambridgeshire County Women's Bowling Association ☎ (01638) 664924

Cricket
Cambridgeshire Cricket Association ☎ (01954) 260295
Cambridge University Cricket Club plays visiting county and touring sides at Fenners Cricket Ground, Gresham Road (main entrance behind Kelsey Kerridge Sports Hall). ☎ 353552/368885
Local teams play on Parker's Piece, and there are many college grounds in the city.

Fencing
Cambridgeshire Fencing Club ☎ 461738

Fitness
Cambridge Garden House Moat House, Club Moativation Health and Fitness Club, Granta Place, Mill Lane, CB2 1RT ☎ 259989
Cambridgeshire Moat House Leisure and Fitness Club, Bar Hill ☎ (01954) 249988
Health and Fitness Club, Forte Posthouse, Bridge Road, Impington ☎ 237000
Long Road Fitness Centre, Long Road ☎ 411583
YMCA, Gonville Place ☎ 356998
See also **Kelsey Kerridge Sports Hall** on the previous page.

Flying
Cambridge Aero Club, Marshall's Airport, Newmarket Road ☎ 373214
Mid-Anglia School of Flying, Marshall's Airport, Newmarket Road ☎ 373261 and (after hours) 373737

Football
Cambridge City Football Club, Milton Road ☎ 357973
Cambridge United Football Club, Abbey Stadium, Newmarket Road ☎ 566500

A Cambridge team that took part in the Heart of the East Millennium Youth Games 1999

A wicket falls in a University cricket match

Golf
Cambridge Lakes Pitch and Putt, Trumpington Road ☎ 324242
Cambridgeshire Moat House Golf Club, Bar Hill, Cambridge ☎ (01954) 249988
Girton Golf Club, Dodford Lane, Girton ☎ 276169
Gog Magog Golf Club, Shelford Bottom, Babraham Road ☎ 246058

Hockey
Cambridge City Hockey Club, Wilberforce Road ☎ 312550

Hunting
Cambridgeshire Harriers, Master Mrs E. Gingell, Horningsea Manor ☎ 860291

Martial arts
Cambridge Academy of Martial Arts ☎ 565020

Rowing clubs
Cambridge '99 ☎ 861343/367521

City of Cambridge ☎ 276412/420400
Rob Roy ☎ (01799) 502742

Rugby Union
Cambridge club, Grantchester Road ☎ 314705
Shelford club, Cambridge Road, Shelford ☎ 245446
Cambridge University club, Grange Road.

Sailing
Cam Sailing ☎ (01354) 655457

Skiing
Bassingbourn Ski Club (dry ski-slope) ☎ (01763) 848114

Squash
Cambridgeshire Squash Rackets Association ☎ 891076
Cambridge Squash and Fitness Club, Histon Road ☎ 358088

Swimming and diving
Cambridge Parkside Pools, Gonville Place ☎ 466100 (recorded message), 466104 (reception)
Abbey Swimming-Pool, Whitehill Road ☎ 213352
Jesus Green Open-Air Swimming-Pool, Jesus Green. Open Jun–Sept 1000–1800. ☎ 457000

Tennis (lawn)
Cambridge Lawn Tennis Association ☎ 323962

Volleyball
Cambridge and District Volleyball Association ☎ 314409

Water polo
City of Cambridge Water Polo Club ☎ 425100

Getting around

Punts on the Mill Pond

lthough Cambridge is a small city on the edge of the fens, it has an excellent transport system. The privately owned Marshall's Airport has flights to Amsterdam for worldwide connections, and Stansted Airport is a half-hour car journey away. There are coach services to Stansted, Heathrow, Luton and Gatwick airports, as there are to London and other major cities. The M11 and A1 roads are within easy reach of Cambridge and the A14, part of which forms the city bypass, connects Cambridge with the M1 and M6 and provides a fast road to the east coast ports of Harwich and Felixstowe. If you are driving a car in Cambridge, please read the paragraph in this section on parking, taking special note of the 'park and ride' details.

National transport

Airports

Stansted Airport is only half an hour away on the M11 motorway. It can also be reached by direct coach services. Stansted Airport information desk ☎ 01279 680500

Cambridge Airport A regional airport equipped with an instrument landing system, associated approach lights and area radar, managed by Marshall Aerospace. ScotAirways have their headquarters here and operate regular flights to Amsterdam and Edinburgh. The airport also handles charter flights on behalf of a number of airlines and in support of the bloodstock industry in Newmarket. GoldAir International – an air taxi company – is also based on the airfield together with two helicopter charter companies, training schools and two flying clubs. Enquiries ☎ 373737
GoldAir International (charter flights) ☎ 373648
ScotAirways ☎ 0870 606 0707
Cambridge Aero Club ☎ 373213
Burman Aviation ☎ 373687
Cambridge Helicopters ☎ 294488
Mid-Anglia School of Flying ☎ 373261

Coach services

There are regular direct services every day to Luton, Stansted, Heathrow and Gatwick airports and to London and many other major cities. For details and bookings call at the **Premier Travel Coach Office** at the **Bus Station** in Drummer Street.
Cambridge Coach Services and **Jetlink** Bookings only ☎ 08705 757747; timetable information ☎ 08705 747777
National Express ☎ 0990 808080
Stagecoach Cambus Operate most of the local bus services ☎ 01223 423554 (Mon–Fri 0700–1900)

Rail services

Cambridge Station. Trains run regularly throughout the day to London's King's Cross and Liverpool Street stations (minimum journey time by express to King's Cross 50 minutes). Credit card bookings available.
National Rail Enquiries, all routes, timetables and information countrywide ☎ 08457 484950 (24 hours)
West Anglia Great Northern travel information hotline ☎ 08457 445522 (24 hours)

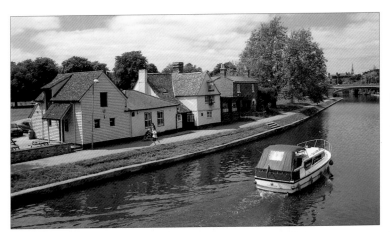

Boating on the Cam

Guide Friday tour bus

Local transport

There are many bus service operators in Cambridge and the environs. For details of services and timetables call at the **Premier Travel Coach Office** in Drummer Street (Mon–Sat 0845–1730) or telephone **Stagecoach Cambus** ☎ 423554 (Mon–Fri 0700–1900) **Cambridge Coach Services** ☎ 236333 **Whippet Coaches** ☎ (01480) 463792

Boat hire (Punts for the River Cam)
Punts are generally available from February to the end of October but, if the weather is suitable, punts are now hireable all through the winter.
Cambridge Chauffeur Punts, The Mill Pond, Silver Street, opposite Queens' College Porters' Lodge. Chauffeured and self-hire punts along the Backs and the upper river to Grantchester. Thai meals by arrangement. ☎ 354176; Fax/24-hr answer machine 359299; mobile 0966 157059.

Scudamore's Boat Yard, Granta Place, The Mill Pond. Chauffeured and self-hire punts and rowing-boats for the Backs and the upper river to Grantchester. Punts are available from the bottom of Mill Lane and from beside the Anchor pub on Silver Street. Punts also available at the Quayside, Bridge Street ☎ 359750; Fax 357565
Tyrrell's Marina, The Quayside, Bridge Street. Chauffeured and self-hire punts. ☎ 01480 413517.

Students trying to make money during the long vacation run their own chauffeured punts from various starting-points along the Backs.

Car hire

A full list of car hire companies is available from the Tourist Information Centre ☎ 322640

Guided walking tours

The Tourist Information Centre organises guided walking tours of Cambridge and the colleges led by Blue Badge Guides. Tours for families and individuals leave the Tourist Information Centre, Wheeler Street, every day. Those coming with a group can book a variety of tours in different languages and for special interests, such as architecture, famous students at Cambridge University and the history of science in Cambridge. In the summer the Tourist Information Centre offers evening drama tours for groups and for individuals, enlivened with costumed characters. For information on guided tours ☎ 457574, or for general information ☎ 322640

Open-top bus tours

Circular open-top bus tours lasting about an hour run every day around Cambridge. The tours include the American Cemetary. The tickets are valid all day so passengers may get off the bus and then reboard it.
Guide Friday (green and cream buses) Tours with live commentary. Taped commentary in six languages is available on selected buses. Tickets can be bought from the Guide Friday office at the Rail Station, from the Tourist Information Centre and from the bus drivers. ☎ or fax 362444

Parking

Cars

Cambridge is an exceptionally difficult city for car drivers. The centre of the city is closed to traffic Mon–Sat 1000–1600. Short-term meter parking is available in some streets near the city centre, and there are a number of short- and long-term multistorey car parks.

Park and ride Cambridge has a park-and-ride scheme that runs Mon–Sat (except Bank Holidays) from car parks on the edge of the city. Parking is free but there is a charge for the bus fare. Up to two children under 14 can travel free when accompanied by an adult. Freephone 0800 243916.

East: on the A1303 Newmarket Road.
North: at Cowley Road near the A14-A10-A1309 junction.
South: on the A1307 near the junction of Hinton Way.
West: on Madingley Road at the M11 north bound Junction 13.

Coach parking

Cowley Road Coach Park, adjacent to the Park and Ride off Milton Road, near the Science Park. A14-A10-A1309 interchange or from city centre. Day rate. Open Mon–Sat 0900–2100, Sun 0900–1900 ☎ 423578.

Madingley Road Park-and-Ride site: A1303 or approach from M11 northbound Junction 13 or from city centre. Limited space. Day rate. Open Mon–Sat 0730–1930 ☎ 321655.

City Football Ground, Milton Road: Approach from A14-A10-A1309 interchange (junction A10/Milton Road) or from city centre. Day rate. Open Sat and Sun only 0730–1930 ☎ 357973. For overnight parking ☎ Stagecoach 423578.

For further information ☎ Tourist Information Centre 457574; Fax 457588

Disabled

The Orange Badge scheme operates in Cambridge. Orange Badge holders may park free of charge and without time limit at on-street parking meters and in pay-and-display spaces. They may also park on single or double yellow lines for up to two hours as long as they are not causing an obstruction. There are parking bays for Orange Badge holders in King's Parade, Guildhall Street, Peas Hill, Regent Street, Napier Street and City Road. Designated spaces are available in the Lion Yard and Grafton Centre multistorey car parks but normal rates will be charged unless otherwise stated. Radar keys may be obtained from the Tourist Information Centre or the reception desk in the Guildhall, Market Hill, during normal opening times.

Motorcycles

There are motorcycle parks close to the city centre on Free School Lane, Botolph Lane, Hobson Street, King Street and Silver Street.

Shop-mobility

The Shop-mobility Scheme provides free electrically powered scooters, wheelchairs and manual wheelchairs for use in the city by people with limited mobility. A member of staff can help you to get in or out of your car. Staff can also meet people at the bus station, city centre bus stops and park-and-ride service. An escort service is available for up to two hours. Please phone the centre you wish to use this facility. The centres are open Mon–Sat 1000–1600, both have a 24-hour answerphone. There are different car-parking arrangements for each centre:
Lion Yard, based on 5th floor of the Lion Yard Car Park. It has an entrance in Tibbs Row, and the main car park entrance can also be used. ☎ 457452.
Grafton Centre, based on 4th floor of East Car Park, entrance East Road. There is a push-button intercom. ☎ 461858

Taxi ranks

Drummer Street Bus Station 0700–0200

Rail Station 24 hours

St Andrew's Street, near the main post office 0700–0200 ☐

Cambridge's park-and-ride scheme runs
from Monday to Saturday from four
locations outside the city

Cycling

Travelling the Cambridge way

Cambridge is a city for cyclists. The streets are narrow, parking is difficult and the centre is closed to traffic during most of the day, so a bicycle is the obvious answer. Thousands of university students – who are not allowed to have cars – ride bicycles to and from lectures, and hundreds of Cambridge residents, from the elderly to the very young, find cycling the ideal antidote to the city's traffic problem. Visiting English-language students have also realised that a bike is the perfect means of transport. But overseas visitors beware — please remember this is England and we ride on the left-hand side of the road! Beware also of thoughtless pedestrians stepping out in front of you. Always padlock your bicycle securely when you leave it.

Certain roads in the city have cycle paths on them, and there are designated cycle routes. When the city centre is closed to cars, some of the streets are also closed to cyclists – you may walk with your bicycle but you must not ride it. Do not cycle the wrong way down one-way streets. There is a bridge specially for cyclists so they can reach distant parts of the city in safety.

Cycle hire

All the shops will charge a deposit and all offer day, week and extended rates for cycle hire.

The Bike Man, Market Square ☎ 0850 814186. Open Mon–Thu.

Cambridge Recycles, 61 Newnham Road (on the roundabout) ☎ 506035. Collection and delivery service. Open every day in summer, Mon–Fri in winter.

The Cycle King, 197–199 Mill Road ☎ 214999. Also offers sales, repairs and clothing.

H. Drake, 56–60 Hills Road ☎ 363468

Geoff's Bikes, 65 Devonshire Road ☎ 365629. Open every day in summer. Mon–Fri in winter.

Mike's Bikes, 28 Mill Road ☎ 312591

University Cycles, 9 Victoria Avenue ☎ 355517

Clare College

Bikes

Useful numbers for cyclists

A 'Cambridge Cycle Route Map' including a guide to getting about Cambridge on a bicycle is available from Cambridgeshire County Council on ☎ 718587

Cycling Officer Cambridgeshire County Council ☎ 717568

Cycle Training for Adults ☎ 712429

Police Headquarters Cambridge (including traffic wardens) ☎ 358966

Potholes and Highway Maintenance Cambridge City Council ☎ 458260

Street Lighting and Traffic Signal Faults Cambridgeshire County Council ☎ 0800 253529

Cyclists' Touring Club, Cambridge ☎ 563414

Cambridge Cycle-Friendly Employers' Scheme ☎ 712429

Cambridge Cycling Campaign, PO Box 204, CB4 3FN ☎ 504095; camcycle@pobox.co.uk

A hotel outside Cambridge city centre
– The Cambridge Quy Mill Hotel
at Stow cum Quy

Accommodation

The Arundel House Hotel, Chesterton Road

Naturally, because of Cambridge's ability to attract visitors worldwide, the city has a wide range of accommodation to offer from homely and comfortable family-run guest houses to opulent hotels. There are excellent conference facilities in the hotels and in many of the colleges. There is also a YMCA and a youth hostel.

All establishments listed below have been classified by the English Tourist Board.

The Cambridge telephone area code is 01223.

Youth hostels in the city
YMCA, Queen Anne House, Gonville Place, CB1 1ND ☎ 356998
Youth Hostel, 97 Tenison Rd, CB1 2AN ☎ 354601

Guesthouses in the city –
£25 per person and under
Acer House, 3 Dean Drive, Holbrook Road, CB1 7SW ☎ 210404; e-mail: carol.dennett @btinternet.com

Ashtrees Guest House, 128 Perne Road, CB1 3RR ☎/Fax 411233

Cambridge Garden House Moat House Hotel

Assisi Guest House, 193 Cherry Hinton Road, Cambridge CB1 7BX ☎ 246648/211466; Fax 412900

Mrs V. Beesley-Schuster, 56 St Barnabas Road, CB1 2DE ☎ 350543; Fax 525725; e-mail: vera @beesley-schuster.demon.co.uk

Brooklands Guest House, 95 Cherry Hinton Road, CB1 7BS ☎/Fax 242035

Dykelands Guest House, 157 Mowbray Road, CB1 7SP ☎ 244300; Fax 566746; e-mail: dykelands@fsbdial.co.uk

El Shaddai, 41 Warkworth Street, CB1 1EG ☎ 327978; Fax 501024; e-mail: pauline.droy@ freeserve.co.uk

Fairways Guest House, 143 Cherry Hinton Road, CB1 7BX ☎ 246063; Fax 212093

Hamden Guest House, 89 High Street, Cherry Hinton CB1 9LU ☎ 413263; Fax 245960

Hills Guest House, 157 Hills Road, CB2 2RJ ☎/Fax 214216

Guesthouses in the city – £35 per person and under

Acorn Guest House, 154 Chesterton Road, CB4 1DA ☎ 353888, (0403) 570096 (mobile); Fax 350527

Alpha-Milton Guest House, 61–63 Milton Road, CB4 1XA ☎ 311625; Fax 565100

Arbury Lodge Guest House, 82 Arbury Road, CB4 2JE ☎ 364319; Fax 566988; e-mail: arburylodge@dtn.ntl.com

Aylesbray Lodge, 5 Mowbray Road, CB1 7SR ☎ 240089; Fax 528678

Benson, 24 Huntingdon Road, CB3 0HH ☎/Fax 311594, (0402) 387859 (mobile)

Cam Guest House, 17 Elizabeth Way, CB4 1DD ☎ 354512; Fax 353164; e-mail: camguesthouse @btinternet.com

Carolina Bed & Breakfast, 148 Perne Road, CB1 3NX ☎/Fax 247015, (0370) 370914 (mobile); e-mail: carolina.amabile@tesco.net

City Haven Guest House, 20 St Margaret's Square, CB1 8AP ☎ 411188; Fax 572078

Cristina's, 47 St Andrew's Road, CB4 1DH ☎ 365855/327700; Fax 365855

De Freville House, 166 Chesterton Road, CB4 1DA ☎ 354993

Dorset House, 35 Newton Road, Little Shelford, CB2 5HL ☎/Fax 844440

Home from Home, 39 Milton Road, CB4 1XA ☎/Fax 323555, (0589) 990698 (mobile); e-mail: Homefromhome@tesco.net

Southampton Guest House, 7 Elizabeth Way, CB4 1DE ☎ 357780; Fax 314297

Springfield House, 16 Horn Lane, Linton CB1 6HT ☎ 891383; Fax 890335

Two Six Four, 264 Hills Road, CB2 2QE ☎ 248369, (0836) 290550 (mobile); Fax 441276; e-mail: dowen@iee.org

Victoria Bed & Breakfast, 57 Arbury Road, CB4 2JB ☎/Fax 350086, (0410) 420855 (mobile); e-mail: vicmaria@globalnet.co.uk

Warkworth House, Warkworth Terrace, CB1 1EE
☎ 363682

Guesthouses in the city –
£45 per person and under
Romanhurst House, 3 Grange Road, CB3 9AS
☎ 352344

Segovia Lodge, 2 Barton Road, Newnham
CB3 9JZ ☎ 354105; Fax 323011

The Suffolk Guest House, 69 Milton Road,
CB4 1XA ☎ 352016; Fax 566816

Hotels in the city
Arundel House Hotel, 53 Chesterton Road,
CB4 3AN ☎ 367701; Fax 367721

Ashley Hotel, 74 Chesterton Road, CB4 1ER
☎ 350059

Cambridge Garden House Moat House Hotel,
Granta Place, Mill Lane, CB2 1RT ☎ 259988;
Fax 316605

Cambridgeshire Moat House, Bar Hill,
Cambridge CB3 8EU ☎ (01954) 249988;
Fax 780010

Crowne Plaza Cambridge, Downing Street,
CB2 3DT ☎ 464466; Fax 464440; e-mail: sales
@cpcam.demon.co.uk

Gonville Hotel, Gonville Place, Cambridge
CB1 1LY ☎ 366611; Fax 315470; e-mail: all@
gonvillehotel.co.uk

Hamilton Hotel, 156 Chesterton Road, CB4 1DA
☎ 365664; Fax 314866

Helen Hotel, 167 Hills Road, CB2 2RJ
☎ 246465; Fax 214406

Lensfield Hotel, 53 Lensfield Road, CB2 1EN
☎ 355017; Fax 312022

Meadowcroft Hotel, Trumpington Road,
CB2 2EX ☎/Fax 303037

Panos Restaurant & Hotel, 154–156 Hills
Road, CB2 2PB ☎ 212958; Fax: 210980

Regent Hotel, 41 Regent Street, CB2 1AB
☎ 351470; Fax 566562; e-mail: reservations@
regenthotel.co.uk

Royal Cambridge Hotel, Trumpington Street,
CB2 1PY ☎ 351631; Fax 352972; e-mail:
royalcambridge@zoffanyhotels.co.uk

Sorrento Hotel, 196 Cherry Hinton Road,
CB1 7AN ☎ 243533; Fax 213463; e-mail:
sorrento-hotel@cb14anfreeserve.co.uk

University Arms Hotel, Regent Street, CB2 1AD
☎ 351241; Fax 461319; e-mail: devere.uniarms
@airtime.co.uk

Hotels and guesthouses outside the city

Archway Guest House, Church Street, Saffron
Walden, Essex CB10 1JW ☎/Fax (01799)
501500, (0780) 1555435 (mobile)

Bridge House, Green End, Stretham, Near Ely,
Cambridgeshire CB6 3LF ☎ (01353) 649212,
(0780) 8869518 (mobile)

Bushel House, 115 The Causeway, Burwell,
Cambridge CB5 0DU ☎ (01638) 602262

Cambridge Quy Mill Hotel, Newmarket Road,
Stow cum Quy, Cambridge CB5 9AG ☎ 293383;
Fax 293770; e-mail: cambridgequy@bestwestern.
co.uk

Church Farm, High Street, Roxton, Bedford
MK44 3EB ☎/Fax (01234) 870234

Denmark House, 58 Denmark Road,
Cottenham, Cambridge CB4 8QS ☎ (01954)
251060, (0411) 905315 (mobile); Fax (01954)
251629; e-mail: denmark.house@tesco.net

Duxford Lodge Hotel, Ickleton Road, Duxford,
Cambridge CB2 4RU ☎ 836444; Fax 832271

Foxhounds, 71 Cambridge Road, Wimpole, Near
Royston, Cambridgeshire SG8 5QD ☎ 207344

Gransden Lodge Farm, Longstowe Road, Little
Gransden, Sandy, Bedfordshire SG19 3EB
☎ (01767) 677365; Fax 677647

Hall Farm, Great Chishill, Near Royston, Hertfordshire SG8 8SH ☎/Fax (01763) 838263

Hill House Farm, 9 Main Street, Coveney, Ely,
Cambridgeshire CB6 2DJ ☎ (01353) 778369

Leys Cottage Bed & Breakfast, 56 Wimpole
Road, Barton, Cambridge CB3 7AB ☎/Fax
262482, (0402) 808562 (mobile)

Manor Farm, Green End, Landbeach, Cambridge
CB4 8ED ☎ 860165

The Meadow House, 2A High Street, Burwell,
Cambridge CB5 0HB ☎ (01638) 741926; Fax
743424

Melbourn Bury, Royston Road, Melbourn,
Royston, Hertfordshire SG8 6DE ☎ (01763)
261151; Fax 262375; e-mail: mazecare@aol.
com

New Manor Farm, Wooley, Huntingdon, Cambridgeshire PE18 0TJ ☎ (01480) 890092

Old Rosemary Branch, 67 Church End, Cherry
Hinton, Cambridge CB1 3LF ☎ 247161; e-mail:
106723.164@compuserve.com

Oliver's Lodge Hotel & Restaurant, Needing-
worth Road, St Ives, Cambridgeshire PE17 4JP
☎ (01480) 463252; Fax 461150; e-mail:
reception@oliverslodge.co.uk

Rockells Farm, Duddenhoe End, Saffron
Walden, Essex CB11 4UY ☎ (01763) 838053;
Fax 837001

Rosendale Lodge, 223 Main Street, Witchford,
Ely, Cambridgeshire CB6 2HT ☎ (01353)
667700; Fax 667799

Spinney Abbey, Wicken, Ely, Cambridgeshire
CB7 5XQ ☎ (01353) 720971

Springfields, Ely Road, Little Thetford, Ely,
Cambridgeshire CB6 3HJ ☎ (01353) 663637;
Fax 663130

Swallow Hotel, Kingfisher Way, Hinchingbrooke
Business Park, Huntingdon PE18 8FL
☎ (01480) 446000; Fax 436329

Wallis Farmhouse, Wallis Farm, 98 Main Street,
Hardwick, Cambridge CB3 7QU ☎ (01954)
210347, (0585) 214297 (mobile); Fax (01954)
210988; e-mail: wallisfarm@mcmail.com

West View, 6 Hardwick Road, Toft, Cambridge CB3 7RQ ☎ 263287/264202

Woodfield House, Madingley Road, Coton, Cambridge CB3 7PH ☎ (01954) 210265; Fax 212650; e-mail: wendy-john@wsadler. freeserve.co.uk

Woodpeckers, 57–61 The Footpath, Coton, Cambridge CB3 7PX ☎ (01954) 210455, (0411) 633618 (mobile); Fax (01954) 210733; e-mail: roy@woodpeckers61.freeserve.co.uk

Yardley's, Orchard Pightle, Hadstock, Cambridge CB1 6PQ ☎/Fax 891822

Campsites

Highfield Touring Park, Long Road, Comberton, Cambridge CB3 7DG. Open Apr–Oct. ☎/Fax 262308

Quiet Waters Caravan Park, Hemingford Abbots, Huntingdon, Cambridgeshire PE18 9AJ. Open Apr–Oct. ☎/Fax (01480) 463405

The YHA Youth Hostel on Tenison Road

Discovering the region

Half-timbered medieval houses in Lavenham, Suffolk

Although millions of visitors converge upon Cambridge just to enjoy the delights of the historic city itself, many do not realise that it is the perfect centre for exploring some of the gentlest and least spoiled countryside in England. With the lonely, romantic fens whose fantastic 'skyscapes' and remarkable light attract countless artists to the north of Cambridge, the city is surrounded on all sides by heritage villages and towns, ancient monuments, and a host of other attractions, all within easy travelling distance. Slightly further afield are the glorious Suffolk wool towns and villages, like Lavenham and Long Melford, largely undisturbed since the Middle Ages and well worth a leisurely visit.

American Cemetery

American Cemetery

American Cemetery, Madingley Road, Coton, Cambridge; 4 miles *6.5 km*. One of the loveliest, most peaceful and certainly most moving places in East Anglia is the American Cemetery, which stands on a beautifully landscaped hillside at Madingley. It commemorates 3,811 American service personnel, including seventeen service-women, who died in the Second World War, and one young airman who died in the Gulf War. The names of 5,126 servicemen who lie in unknown graves are inscribed on the Memorial Wall. The cemetery is open daily, including Christmas, 16 Apr–30 Sept 0800–1800, 1 Oct–15 Apr 0800–1700. ☎ (01954) 210350

Historic towns

Historic towns within quick reach of Cambridge include ...

Bury St Edmunds, 29 miles *47 km* E. This is a bustling Suffolk market town, with a cathedral and the remains of a great Norman abbey where the barons met before going on to Runnymede for the signing of Magna Carta. Here was the shrine of St Edmund, last Saxon king, slaughtered by the Vikings. The town is crowded with historic buildings and its exquisite Regency Theatre Royal is still thriving. The Nutshell Inn is said to be the smallest in Britain. Bury has two open markets on Wed and Sat; early closing Thu.

Great Ouse River and Ely Cathedral

Abbey Gate, Bury St Edmunds

Ely, 16 miles *26 km* N. Small fenland market town dominated by its magnificent cathedral with its unique fourteenth-century octagon and superb monastic buildings. Oliver Cromwell's House is now a themed tourist information and visitor centre. There is constant river activity. Market day is on Thursday; early closing is on Tuesday.

Huntingdon, 16 miles *26 km* W. Birthplace of Oliver Cromwell (1599); his old school is now the Cromwell Museum. Originally the county town of Huntingdonshire, one of the smallest English counties , it has attracted much new commerce and industry and has a popular National Hunt racecourse.

Lavenham and the Suffolk 'Wool Towns', 36 miles *58 km* E. Built with wealth from the medieval wool and cloth industry, the village of Lavenham and nearby **Long Melford** 33 miles *53 km* are little-changed over the centuries, and each place claims it has the finest church in the county of Suffolk. Lavenham has a wealth of

half-timbered buildings — its sixteenth-century Guildhall, overlooking the market-place, is one of the country's finest Tudor buildings. Long Melford, with its wide main street housing many antique shops, also has Melford Hall (NT) and Kentwell Hall, both splendid red-brick Tudor mansions.

St Ives Bridge Chapel

Newmarket, 13 miles *21 km* E. Headquarters of the British thoroughbred horse-racing industry. Visit early in the morning to watch racehorses training on the gallops. Newmarket has the National Stud and the National Horse-Racing Museum and is the home of the Jockey Club. Its two racecourses are among the world's finest. There are over 5,000 horses in training and on stud farms in the Newmarket area. Market days Tuesday and Saturday; early closing Wednesday.

Saffron Walden, 15 miles *24 km* SE. Unspoiled and famed for the pargeting (decorative plaster-work) on many of its historic buildings. On the Common is a rare earth maze and a restored hedge maze in Bridge End Gardens. Its name is from the saffron made in medieval days from crocuses grown in the town. Audley End House is nearby. Market days Tuesday and Saturday; early closing Thursday.

St Ives, 13 miles *21 km* W. Like Ely and Huntingdon, St Ives is also a historic riverside town. On its fifteenth-century bridge over the Great Ouse is one of only three remaining bridge chapels in the country. Cromwell's short stay in the town is commemorated by a splendid statue in the market place. Market days are Monday and Friday; early closing Thursday.

... and Grantchester, 2¹/₂ *4 km* SW. Of all the attractive villages near Cambridge the best-known is, of course, Grantchester, just outside the city boundary near Trumpington. Immortalised by Rupert Brooke who lived in the Old Vicarage, it has the river with a pool where Lord Byron swam, charming thatched cottages, inns, the church ('Stands the Church clock at ten to three?'). The church clock now works but there is 'honey still for tea' in the Orchard Tea Gardens.

Historic houses

Anglesey Abbey (NT), Lode, Cambridgeshire; 6 miles *10 km* NE. Thirteenth-century abbey with Tudor and modern additions. Home of Lord and Lady Fairhaven. A superb 100-acre *40.5-ha* garden and water mill; Fairhaven collection of paintings and furniture; fascinating clocks. House open Mar–Oct Wed–Sun and Bank hols 1300–1700. Gardens open all year: Jul–Sept daily 1030–1730; other times Wed–Sun and Bank hols 1030–dusk. ☎ 811200

Audley End House (EH), Saffron Walden, Essex; 14 miles *23 km* SE. Palatial Jacobean mansion set in 'Capability' Brown parkland. Robert Adams rooms and furniture. House remodelled in eighteenth to nineteenth centuries. Open Apr–Sept Wed–Sun and Bank Hol Mon: House 1300–1800, last admission 1700; Grounds 1100–1800. Guided tours of house and/or gardens by prior arrangement. ☎ information (01799) 522399; office (01799) 522842

Burghley House, Stamford, Lincolnshire; 43 miles *69 km* NW. Most magnificent house of the first Elizabethan age. Ancestral home of the Marquess of Exeter. Splendid furniture, fire-places, paintings, porcelain and silver. Park. House open Apr–Oct daily 1100–1630, closed one day in Sept for the Burghley Horse Trials. Please check. ☎ (01780) 752451

Old Kitchen, Burghley House

Anglesey Abbey Gardens

Ickworth House (NT), Ickworth, near Bury St Edmunds, Suffolk; 33 miles *53km* E. This is a Rotunda house begun in 1795 and containing a splendid collection of pictures including those by Gainsborough, Titian and Velasquez. Georgian silver. 'Capability' Brown Park and Italian garden. House open Mar–Oct Tue, Wed, Fri, Sat, Sun and Bank holidays 1300–1700. Garden open Mar–Oct daily 1000–1700, Nov–Mar 1000–1600. Park open daily 0700–1900. ☎ (01284) 735270

Wimpole Hall (NT), Arrington, Cambridgeshire; 8 miles *13 km* SW. Largest country-house in Cambridgeshire, former home of Rudyard Kipling's daughter. Eighteenth-century, landscaped park. Home Farm with rare breeds, museum, children's corner, adventure playground. Hall open Mar–Nov Tue–Thu, Sat, Sun, Bank hols 1300–1700. Farm open all year Sat, Sun 1030–1700, Mar–Nov Tue–Thu, Sat, Sun, Bank Hol Mon 1030–1700. ☎ 207257

Woburn Abbey, Woburn, Bedfordshire; 44 miles *71 km* SW. Woburn Abbey is the family home of the Dukes of Bedford and, with its Safari Park in the 3,000-acre *1,214-ha* grounds, is perhaps the best-known of all the English stately homes open to the public. The eighteenth-century mansion has splendid state apartments and superb collections of art, porcelain, plate and furniture. Abbey open Mar–Oct daily 1100–last admission 1600, closed Nov and Dec, open Jan–Mar Sat, Sun and Bank hols. Safari Park open Mar–Oct daily 1000–1700, winter weekends 1100–1500 weather permitting. ☎ (01525) 290666

Gardens, orchards, vineyards and country parks

Anglesey Abbey (NT), Lode, Cambridgeshire; 6 miles *10 km* NE. Created this century from desolate fenland, the Abbey's gardens are recognised as being the finest in the county and the last great formal country-house garden. (See under Historic houses, Anglesey Abbey.)

Bridge End Gardens, Saffron Walden, Essex; 15 miles *24 km* SE. This is a Victorian garden with particularly fine trees. Open daily 0900–dusk.

Chilford Hundred Vineyard, Chilford Hall, Linton, Cambridgeshire; 12 miles *19 km* SE. Winery set in old buildings, where the whole process of winemaking is explained. There is a vineyard, café, shop and sculptures. Open daily 1100–1730. Guided tours available by appointment. ☎ 892641

Coton Orchard and Vineyard, Madingley Road, Cambridge. 2 miles, *3 km* NW. Orchard, vineyard and garden centre producing its own pressed and bottled wine and apple juice; 'pick-your-own' fruit, licensed coffee shop. There are disabled facilities. Mon–Fri 0900–1730, Sat 0900–1830, Sun 1000–1630. ☎ (01954) 210234; Fax 212332.

Docwra's Manor Garden, Shepreth, Cambridgeshire; 6½ miles *10 km* SW. Walled gardens around eighteenth-century house, unusual plants and twentieth-century folly. Plants for sale. Open all year Wed, Fri 1000–1600; first Sun April–Oct 1400–1600. ☎ Manor (01763) 260235; Gardens (01763) 261557/261473

Hinchingbrooke Country Park, Huntingdon, Cambridgeshire; 16 miles *26 km* W. Watersports, countryside events, walks in 156 acres *63 ha* of woods, lakes and meadows. Hinchingbrooke House with its strong Cromwellian associations is open May–Aug Sun 1400–1700.

Milton Country Park, Milton, Cambridge; 3 miles *5 km* N, a mixture of woodland, grass and water areas with a network of surfaced paths over two miles in length suitable for bicycles and wheelchairs as well as for walkers. There is a marked trail for horseriders. Wildlife, fishing (with an annual Angling Club licence). NO swimming! Open daily, except Christmas Day, from 0800. Closing times vary. ☎ 420060.

Mills

Bourn Windmill, Bourn, Cambridgeshire; 8 miles *13 km* W. Possibly oldest pre-Civil War post mill in England. Normally open last Sun in month Mar–Sept 1400–1700. ☎ 243830.

Burwell Windmill, Cambridgeshire; 10 miles *16 km* NE. Stephens' Mill, 1820, extensively restored by Burwell Windmill Trust. Open in conjunction with Burwell Museum Easter–Sept Thu and Sun 1400–1700. ☎ (01638) 741689

Downfield Windmill, Soham, Cambridgeshire; 16 miles *26 km* NE. Built 1726, the windmill still produces flour for visitors and local shops. Open all year Sun and Bank Hol Mon 1100–1700, closed 25 Dec–2 Jan. ☎ (01353) 720333

Hinxton Water Mill, Hinxton, Cambridgeshire; 6 miles *10 km* SW. Restored seventeenth-century water mill now grinding flour. Open single days during May, June, July and Sept 1430–1700.

Houghton Mill (NT), Houghton, Cambridgeshire; 15 miles *24 km* E. Much of the nineteenth-century machinery of this large, wooden-built mill on the River Ouse is still intact and some in working order. Open Easter–Oct Sat, Sun, Bank Hol Mon 1400–1730, end June–Sept also open Mon–Wed 1400–1730. ☎ (01480) 301494

Lode Water Mill, Lode, Cambridgeshire; 6 miles *10 km* NE. Part of the Anglesey Abbey estate (see under Historic Houses). ☎ 811200

Shade Windmill, Soham, Cambridgeshire; 12 miles *19 km* NE. Privately owned but can be viewed from the road.

Swaffham Prior, Cambridgeshire; 8 miles *13 km* NE. Swaffham Prior has two windmills (and two churches in the same churchyard!). The 1850s Tower Mill is restored and again making flour.

Royston Cave

Open for sale of flour any reasonable time. Open otherwise by appointment only ☎ (01638) 741009. Opposite is a restored smock mill. Not open to the public.

Wicken Fen Windpump, Wicken, Cambridge-shire; 14 miles *23 km* NE. Working windpump in the last undrained portion of the Fens. Open all year daily from dawn to dusk except 25 Dec. Parties must book. ☎ (01353) 720274

Ancient monuments and buildings

Buckden Towers, Buckden, Cambridgeshire; 19 miles *31 km* NW. This former moated ecclesiastical palace of the bishops of Lincoln has a mainly fifteenth-century complex of buildings with the Great Tower, King's Room and Inner Gatehouse. Church and courtyard open during daylight hours, buildings and grounds by appointment. Bookshop and information centre open Wed–Sun 1200–1700. ☎ (01480) 810344

Bury St Edmunds Abbey, Bury St Edmunds, Suffolk; 29 miles *47 km* E. Remains of the vast Norman abbey in beautiful gardens. Open daily.

Denny Abbey, (EH) Waterbeach, Cambridge-shire; 5 miles *8 km* N. This Grade 1 listed Abbey was founded in the twelfth century as a Bene-dictine church. Later it housed Knights Templar, the Countess of Pembroke, (foundress of Pembroke College, Cambridge) and Franciscan nuns. Became a farmhouse in the sixteenth century. Joint admission with the Farmland Museum (see Museums). Open Mar–Oct daily 1200–1700. ☎ 860489

Ely Cathedral, Ely, Cambridgeshire; 16 miles *26 km* N. 'The Great Ship of the Fens', Ely Cathedral, one of the finest in England, is gloriously crowned by its Octagon. There is a Stained Glass Museum and Brass Rubbing

Centre, and guided tours are available in summer. Open British Summer Time daily 0700–1900; winter Mon–Sat 0730–1800, Sun 0730–1700. No facilities — shop, guided tours or refreshments — on 1 April and 25, 26 Dec. ☎ (01353) 667735

Flag Fen, Fengate, Peterborough. 39 miles *63 km* N. Important continuing Bronze Age excavations. Bronze Age landscape, round-houses and primitive animals. Preservation Hall with 3,000-year-old remains. Open daily 1100–1700, closed Dec 25, 26. ☎ (01733) 313414.

Grimes Graves (EH), Lynford, Norfolk; 35 miles *56 km* NE. Unique series of 4,000-year-old neo-lithic flint mines. Of more than 300 pits and shafts, one is open to the public – 30 feet *9.1 m* deep with seven galleries radiating from it. There is a site exhibition. Open daily April–Oct 1000–1300, 1400–1800; Nov–Mar Wed–Sun 1000–

The Lodge – RSPB headquarters

1300, 1400–dusk, closed 24, 25 Dec and 1 Jan. ☎ (01842) 810656

Hedingham Castle, Castle Hedingham, Essex; 29 miles *47 km*. The square Norman keep, built in 1140, dominates the village. Banqueting Hall

Statue of Mill Reef at the National Stud in Newmarket

with a Minstrels' Gallery and a Tudor bridge built in 1496 to replace the drawbridge. Woodland and lakeside walks. Open week before Easter–Oct 1000–1700. ☎ (01787) 460261

Isleham Priory Church, Isleham, Cambridgeshire; 13 miles *21 km* NE. Remains of the Norman church. Open 'any reasonable time'.

Ramsey Abbey (NT), Ramsey, Cambridgeshire; 20 miles *32 km* NW. Twelfth-century lady chapel and Tudor house. Open by appointment only. ☎ (01487) 813285

Ramsey Abbey Gatehouse, Ramsey, Cambridgeshire; 20 miles *32 km* NW. Ruins of the fifteenth-century gatehouse. Open April–Oct daily 1000–1700. ☎ (01263) 733471

Royston Cave, Melbourn Street, Royston, Hertfordshire; 14 miles *23 km* S. Strange, bell-shaped chamber hollowed out of chalk under Melbourn Street with medieval wall-carvings. Of unknown origin, it is thought to have been used by the Knights Templar in the thirteenth century. Open Easter to Sept Sat, Sun and Bank Hol Mon 1430–1700. ☎ (01763) 245484

St Ives Bridge Chapel, St Ives, Cambridgeshire; 13 miles *21 km* W. Built in the 1420s in the middle of the bridge over the River Ouse, this is a perfect example of a rare type of building. Open all year, any time, keys from the Norris Museum (St Ives) or local shops. ☎ (01480) 465101

Wandlebury Ring Fort, near Babraham, Cambridgeshire; 4 miles *6 km* S. Circular Iron Age encampment, 110 acres *44.5 ha* of parkland, walks, nature trail. Open daily. ☎ 243830

Nature reserves, animals and wildlife

Fowlmere Reserve (RSPB), Fowlmere, Cambridgeshire; 5 miles *8 km* SW. Fen nature reserve with hides and trail. Open all year.

Wood Green Animal Shelter

Hayley Wood, Gamlingay, Cambridgeshire; 16 miles *26 km* SW. Ancient woodland, oak, ash, hazel, bluebells and other spring flowers.

Home Farm (NT), Wimpole Hall, Arrington, Cambridgeshire; 8 miles *13 km* SW. Approved rare-breeds centre and farm museum. Suffolk punch horse wagon rides. Open Sat, Sun all year 1300–1700, Mar–Oct Sat, Sun, Tue–Thu, Bank Hol Mon 1030–1700

Linton Zoo, Linton, Cambridgeshire; 10 miles *16 km* SE. Intimate zoo in 16 acres *6.5 ha*, from big cats to tarantulas. Open daily, not 25 Dec, 1000–dusk. ☎ 891308

The Lodge (RSPB), Sandy, Bedfordshire; 22 miles *35 km* SW. Headquarters of the Royal Society for the Protection of Birds, The Lodge has 106 acres *43 ha* of woods, heath, grassland, nature trails and a lake with a hide. The reserve is open daily throughout the year 0900–2100 or sunset. ☎ (01767) 680551

The National Stud, Newmarket, Suffolk; 13 miles *21 km* W. Formed during the First World War, the National Stud moved to its present 500-acre *202-ha* site on the edge of Newmarket in 1963. It is now one of the principal stallion stations in Britain with eight top-class stallions.

The National Stud organises 75-minute tours during which visitors are 'introduced' to the stallions before meeting the mares and foals. Some foals will be only a day old. Tour times from Mar–Aug: weekdays 1115 and 1430, Saturdays 1115, Sundays 1430. ☎ (01638) 663464 in office hours or tour times Sat–Sun.

Ouse Washes, near Manea, Cambridgeshire; 25 miles *40 km* NE. Most important inland site in Britain for wintering ducks and swans. Observation hides, access from reserve car-park. Open all year.

Wicken Fen (NT), Wicken, Cambridgeshire; 14 miles *23 km* NE. 600 acres *243 ha* of last undrained fen; birds, butterflies, nature trails. Open daily dawn–dusk, Visitor Centre 0900–1700. ☎ (01353) 720274

Wildlife and Wetland Trust Centre, Welney, Cambridgeshire; 28 miles *45 km* N. Hides overlook 900 acres *364 ha* of washes with a huge bird population. Special evening visits Nov–Feb to watch floodlit swans feeding. Open daily 1000–1700, not 25 or 26 Dec. ☎ (01353) 860711

Willersmill Wildlife Park, Shepreth, Cambridgeshire; 6½ *10 km* SW. Wildlife park and animal shelter with wolves, monkeys, owls, otters and large fish. Open summer 1000–1800, winter 1000–dusk. ☎ (01763) 262226

Woburn Abbey Safari Park, Woburn, Bedfordshire; 44 miles *71 km* SW. Set in the 3,000-acre *1,214-ha* grounds of the Abbey, the Safari Park has many different species, including lions, tigers, bears and monkeys roaming free. Adventure playground and boating-lake. Open Mar–Oct 1000–1700 and weekends through winter 1100–1500. ☎ (01525) 290666

Wood Green Animal Shelter, Godmanchester, Cambridgeshire; 16 miles *26 km* E. 50-acre *20-ha* site housing unwanted dogs, cats and other small animals. Open all year 0900–1500. ☎ (01480) 830014

Walks, long and short ...

Descriptions of the following walks in detail can be obtained from the Tourist Information Centre, Wheeler Street, Cambridge ☎ 322640, unless otherwise stated.

Bishop's Way, Ely, Cambridgeshire; 16 miles *26 km* N. A 7- to 9-mile *11- to 14.5-km* circular walk on ancient tracks north of Ely.

Clopton Way, Wimpole, Cambridgeshire; 8 miles *13 km* SW. A walk of 10 miles *16 km* from Wimpole to Gamlingay, using prehistoric trackway. Links in with Wimpole Way and Greensand Ridge Walk.

Devil's Dyke, from either Reach (10 miles *16 km* NE) or Stetchworth (11 miles *18 km* E), Cambridgeshire. A defensive fortification ditch of AD 500, it runs from open chalk and fenland at Reach to thick woodland at Stetchworth. About 7½ miles *12 km*. Walk from either direction.

Ely Easy Access Trail, Ely, Cambridgeshire; 16 miles *26 km* N. Trail of 2 miles *3.2 km* along the river and nature trail for all ages and abilities. Leaflet available from Cambridgeshire County Council. ☎ 317111

Grafham Water Circular Ride, Grafham, Cambridgeshire; 22 miles *35 km* E. A 13-mile *21-km* circular ride round the reservoir. Leaflet available from Cambridgeshire County Council. ☎ 317111

Ouse Valley Way, Eaton Socon–Earith, Cambridgeshire; 17 miles *27 km* E. A 26-mile *42-km* river-valley walk along the Great Ouse from Eaton Socon to Earith. Details from Huntingdon Tourist Information Centre. ☎ (01480) 425831

Roman Road Circular Walk, Stapleford, Cambridgeshire; 5 miles *8 km* SE. From Stapleford along the River Granta up to Copley Hill and along the Roman Road through Wandlebury; about 6 miles *9.6 km*.

Cromwell Museum, Huntingdon

Norris Museum, St Ives

Roman Road Walk, Linton, Cambridgeshire; 10 miles *16 km* SE. A 6½-mile *10.5-km* circular walk from Linton to Hildersham along a Roman trackway.

Shepreth Riverside Walk, Shepreth, Cambridge-shire; 6½ miles *10 km* SW. Walk through tree-fringed meadows between Shepreth and Barrington. Leaflet available from Cambridge-shire County Council. ☎ 717111

Wandlebury Country Park Nature Trails, near Babraham, Cambridgeshire; 4 miles *6 km* S. Three short walks mainly through woodland round Wandlebury Ring Iron Age fort.

Wicken Walks (NT), Wicken, Cambridgeshire; 14 miles *23 km* NE. Walks through fascinating cross-sections of original fen landscape.

Wimpole Way, Wimpole, Cambridgeshire; 8 miles *13 km* SW. A 13-mile *21-km* walk from Cambridge to Wimpole Hall through fields and woods.

Museums

Burwell Museum Trust, Mill Close, Burwell, Cambridgeshire; 10 miles *16 km* NE. A smithy and wheelwright's shop are in this village museum housed in a rebuilt eighteenth-century barn. Open all year, Sun; April–Oct also Bank hols, 1400–1700.

Cromwell Museum, Grammar School Walk, Huntingdon, Cambridgeshire; 16 miles *26 km* W. Both Oliver Cromwell and Samuel Pepys went to school in this building. Cromwellian documents, portraits, artefacts. Open April–Oct Tue–Fri 1100–1300, 1400–1700; Sat–Sun 1100–1300, 1400–1600; Nov–Mar Tue–Fri 1300–1600, Sat 1100–1300, 1400–1600; Sun 1400–1600. ☎ (01480) 425830

Ely Museum at The Old Gaol, Market Street, Ely, Cambridgeshire; 16 miles *26 km* N. Historical story of the Isle of Ely and the Cathedral city at its heart from the Ice Age to modern times. Open Tue–Sun and Bank Hol Mon 1030–1630 ☎ (01353) 666655

The Farmland Museum, Waterbeach, Cambridge; 5 miles *8 km* N. Cambridgeshire farming and village life, especially 1940s–50s, in historic farm buildings. Joint admission with Denny Abbey (see Ancient Monuments and Buildings). Open Mar–Oct daily 1200–1700 ☎ 860988

Imperial War Museum, Duxford (see below under 'Machinery and transport'.

National Horseracing Museum, High Street, Newmarket, Suffolk; 13 miles *21 km* E. Develop-ment of horses and racing shown in fine paint-ings, bronzes, trophies and memorabilia and a practical racing gallery: exhibitions by the British Sporting Art Trust. Equine tours arranged. Open Apr–Oct Tue–Sun 1000–1700, but in July and Aug daily 1000–1700 ☎ (01638) 667333

Stained Glass Museum, Ely Cathedral

Norris Museum, Broadway, St Ives, Cambridgeshire; 13 miles *21 km* W. This is the museum for Huntingdonshire. Archaeological remains, special Civil War and French prisoner-of-war displays. Exhibits from every part of the old county. Open Jan–April, Oct–Dec Mon–Fri 1000–1300, 1400–1600, Sat 1000–1200; May–Sept Mon–Fri 1000–1300, 1400–1700, Sat 1000–1200, 1400–1700, Sun 1400–1700, closed Easter, 24–26 Dec, 1–3 Jan. ☎ (01480) 497314

Ramsey Rural Museum, Cemetery Road, Ramsey, Cambridgeshire; 22 miles *35 km* NW. Old fen farm implements, Victoriana, chemist's shop and a cobbler's. Open Easter–Sept Sun, Thu 1400–1700. Closed Easter. ☎ (01487) 815715

Royston and District Museum, Lower King Street, Royston, Hertfordshire; 10 miles *16 km* SW. Local history museum. Fine modern ceramics. Open all year Wed, Thu, Sat 1000–1700, Sun and Bank Hol Mon 1400–1700. ☎ (01763) 242587

Saffron Walden Museum, Museum Street, Saffron Walden, Essex; 15 miles *24 km* SE. A hundred and fifty years old, it has Norman castle ruins in grounds, an ancient Egyptian room, archaeology and early history, geology, local history. Open Mar–Oct Mon–Sat 1000–1700, Sun 1400–1700, Bank hols 1400–1700; Nov–Feb Mon–Sat 1000–1630, Sun 1400–1630, Bank hols 1400–1630, closed 24 and 25 Dec. ☎ (01799) 510333

Shuttleworth Collection, Biggleswade (see below under 'Machinery and transport').

Stained Glass Museum, Cathedral, Ely, Cambridgeshire; 16 miles *26 km* N. Seventy-four panels on display, there are examples of stained glass from the thirteenth-century to modern glass. Stained-glass-making explained. Open all year Sun 1200–1500; Sat and Bank hols 1030–1630; Apr–Oct Mon–Fri 1030–1600; closed 1 Apr, 25 Dec. ☎ (01353) 667735/6

Machinery and transport

Audley End Miniature Railway, Audley End, Essex; 14 miles *23 km* SE. Steam and diesel locomotives in 10¼"-gauge running through attractive countryside. Open Apr–Oct Sat, Sun, Bank Hol Mon and every day during school holidays, with special days including Santa specials 1400–1700. ☎ (01799) 541354

Imperial War Museum, Duxford, Cambridgeshire; 13 miles *21 km* SW. The country's largest collection of military and civil aircraft is housed on this former Battle of Britain airfield. The Land warfare Hall houses tanks and artillery and the newly opened American Air Museum contains the finest display of historic American aircraft outside the US. Special exhibitions, ride simulator, pleasure-flying summer weekends, restaurant, adventure playground. All year Mar–Oct 1000–1800; Oct–Mar 1000–1600. ☎ 835000

Second World War Spitfire at the
Imperial War Museum, Duxford

Cambridge Fine Art

Prickwillow Engine Museum, Main Street, Prickwillow, Cambridgeshire; 18 miles *29 km* NE. Mirrlees Bickerton and Day diesel, Vicker-Petter two-cylinder two-stroke diesel and others. Open May–Sept daily 1100–1700; Mar–Apr, Oct–Nov Sat, Sun and Bank hols 1100–1600, closed Dec–Feb. For details of special 'run' days ☎ (01353) 688360. When the museum is closed ☎ (01353) 688230

Shuttleworth Collection, Old Warden Aerodrome, Biggleswade, Bedfordshire; 23 miles *37 km*. The aerodrome has a historic collection of old aeroplanes, some of which are unique, including a 1909 Bleriot and 1942 Spitfire, as well as collections of cars, dating from 1898, and bicycles, many of which are in working order. Flying-displays on some weekends. Open daily Apr–Oct 1000–1600; Nov–Mar 1000–1500, closed 22 Dec–1 Jan. ☎ (01767) 627288

Stretham Beam-engine, Green End, Stretham, Cambridgeshire; 11 miles *18 km* N. Preserved intact, the steam beam-engine used to drive the massive scoop wheel of the Stretham old engine

Twentypence Pottery

built in 1831 as part of the programme to drain the fens. Open Easter–Sept weekends and Bank Hol Mon 1130–1700. ☎ (01353) 649210

Craft workshops and galleries

Abington Pottery, High Street, Little Abington, Cambridgeshire; 6 miles *10 km* SE. Ceramics, handwoven rugs, glass candles, toys. Open 0900–1800 daily. ☎ 891723

Laurence Broderick, sculptor, Thane Studios, Waresley, Cambridgeshire; 16 miles *26 km* W. Bronze and stone, nudes and wildlife. Open by appointment. ☎ (01767) 650444

Bulbeck Foundry, Reach Road, Burwell, Cambridgeshire; 10 miles *16 km* NE. Reproduction eighteenth-century English lead statuary, fountains, urns, cisterns. Specialist repairs and casting. Open Mon–Fri 0830–1300, 1400–1730. ☎ (01638) 743153

Cambridge Brass-Rubbing Centre, The Round Church, Cambridge. Over 100 facsimiles, taken off the original memorials, are available for rubbing. Individuals, families and groups can be catered for. ☎ (01831) 839261

Cambridge Fine Art, Church Street, Little Shelford, Cambridgeshire; 4 miles *6 km* S. Oil paintings and prints between 1750 and 1930. Paintings for sale. Open Mon–Sat 1000–1800 and by appointment Sun afternoons. ☎ 842866

Crafty Needle, Meldreth Road, Whaddon, Cambridgeshire; 8 miles *13 km* SW. Specialist needlework centre set in 2 acres *0.8 ha* of gardens. Accessories for embroidery, cross-stitch tapestry and quilting. Evening group visits. Open Mon–Sat 1000–1700, Sun 1300–1700. ☎ 208103

Old Fire Engine House, St Mary's Street, Ely, Cambridgeshire; 16 miles *26 km* N. Well-known restaurant with art exhibitions throughout the year. Gallery open Mon–Fri 1030–2230, Sat 1030–1730, Sun 1230–1730. Closed Bank hols. Restaurant open: coffee 1030–1130 Mon–Sat; lunch 1230–1400 every day; tea 1530–1730 Mon–Sat, 1600–1730 Sun; dinner 1930–2100 Mon–Sat. Closed Bank hols. ☎ (01353) 662582

Seven Springs Pottery, Mill Street, Ashwell, Cambridgeshire; 14 miles *23 km* SW. Pottery, craft shop. Open Mon, Tue, Fri, Sat, Sun 1000–1300, and 1400–1700. ☎ (01462) 742152

Twentypence Pottery, Twentypence Road, Wilburton, Cambridgeshire; 12 miles *19 km* N. Woodturning, glazed stoneware, pots, furniture. Open daily 0900–1800, later on Saturdays. ☎ (01353) 741353 ☐

ELY

THE CATHEDRAL CITY IN THE FENS

VISIT this historic City where the medieval buildings make a perfect setting for the magnificent Norman Cathedral.

- The beautifully restored former home of Oliver Cromwell
- Ely Museum depicting the colourful history of the city
- A large riverside antique centre
- Thursday general market
- Saturday craft and antique market

For further information, please contact:

Ely Tourist Information Centre,
Oliver Cromwell's House,
29 St Mary's Street
Ely, Cambs.
Telephone: 01353 662062

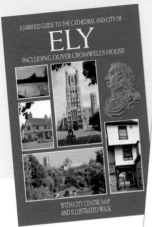

A Jarrold Guide to the Cathedral and City of Ely including Oliver Cromwell's House

with city centre map and illustrated walk

A comprehensive full-colour illustrated guide for visitors covering:

History; Ely Cathedral and Precincts; Oliver Cromwell; Museums and Attractions, including Oliver Cromwell's House, the Stained Glass Museum, the Ely Museum, shopping and eating out;The Fens and the Surrounding Area, including a history of drainage work in the fens and the sluices at Denver, with brief details of the other attractions in and around this Fenland centre, such as Anglesey Abbey, Welney nature reserve and Newmarket with its horse-racing.

Information panels highlight subjects of special local interest, including Hereward the Wake, the Roman villa at Stonea, the Stretham steam-engine, Dorothy Sayers, and the Soham disaster of 1944.

Also includes:
- list of all attractions in and around Ely
- phone numbers and opening times
- full-page map to the city centre
- illustrated walk through the city with its own map

32 pages • 80 illustrations
245x168 mm • £2.50

Available from all good booksellers

Other Jarrold City Guides

Bath (also in French and German), *Cambridge* (also in French, German, Italian, Japanese and Spanish), *Canterbury* (also in Dutch, French, German, Italian, Japanese and Spanish), *Cardiff* (also in French and German), *Chester, Colchester* (also in French in German), *Exeter* (also in French and German), *Lincoln, Norwich* (also in French and German), *Oxford* (also in French, German, Italian, Japanese and Spanish), *Salisbury* (also in French and German), *York* (also in French and German)

English language schools

Students of all ages and abilities come from all over the world to study English in Cambridge. A number of permanent language schools here are recognised by the British Council. During their course of study many students stay with local families and thus learn not only our language but also about our customs — and food! Many students forge life-long friendships with their 'families'.

Anglo-World Cambridge, 75 Barton Road ☎ 357702
Bell School of Languages, 1 Red Cross Lane – off Hills Road ☎ 247242

Cambridge Academy of English, 65 High Street, Girton ☎ 277230
Cambridge Centre for English Studies, Guildhall Chambers, Guildhall Place ☎ 357190

Cambridge Centre for Languages, Sawston Hall, Sawston ☎ 835099

Cambridge Eurocentre, GCE Dept, 62 Bateman Street ☎ 353607

Cambridge School of Languages, 119 Mill Road ☎ 312333/312346

EF International School of English, 221 Hills Road ☎ 240020

Embassy CES Newnham, 8 Grange Road ☎ 311344

International Language Academy, 12–13 Regent Terrace ☎ 350519

Language Studies International, 41 Tenison Road ☎ 361783

New School of English, 52 Bateman Street ☎ 358089

OISE Cambridge, 81–83 Hills Road, Cambridge CB2 1PG ☎ 321084; Fax 355079

Studio School of English, 6 Salisbury Villas, Station Road, Cambridge CB1 2JF ☎ 369701; Fax 314944 ☐

An outdoor class at the Bell School

Useful information

Annual events

January

Pantomime

Lent Term begins

February

Anglesey Abbey Snowdrop Weekend

Rag Week

The Lent Bumps

March

Lent Term ends

Wimpole Hall Lambing Weekends

Anglesey Abbey Open Day

National Science Week

University Boat Race rowed on the River Thames

April

Thriplow Daffodil Week

Easter Term begins

Wimpole Home Farm Lambing Weekends

Easter Fair, Midsummer Common

May

Reach Fair

Stilton Cheese-Rolling, Stilton

Spalding Flower Festival

Cambridge Mayor-Making

Mildenhall Air Fête

Cambridge Beer Festival

American Cemetery Memorial Day

June

Strawberry Fair, Midsummer Common

University of Cambridge Honorary Degree Day (sometimes held in July)

May Week

College May Balls

'Colleges' May 'Bumps'

University of Cambridge Degree Days

Easter Term ends

Midsummer Fair, Midsummer Common

Shakespeare Festival

Cambridge Folk Festival

East of England Show, Peterborough

Rose Fair, Wisbech

July

Shakespeare Festival

World Pea-Shooting Championships, Witcham

Duxford Air Show

Ely Folk Weekend

Open Studios (local artists and crafts people open their studios free)

Summer Recitals

East of England Show, Peterborough

Wimpole Hall, Open Air Summer Music Festival with Fireworks

Cambridge Raft Race

Q 103 Radio Fringe Arts Festival

'Summer in the City' with fireworks, Parker's Piece

London to Cambridge Cycle Ride, Midsummer Common

Cambridge Folk Festival, Cherry Hinton Hall

City Rowing Bumps

August

Shakespeare Festival

Summer Recitals

Fenland Country Fair, Stow cum Quy, near Cambridge on Bank Holiday Sunday and Monday

September

Wimpole Hall, Heavy Horse Show

Burghley Horse Trials, Burghley House and Park

Duxford Airfield Family Air Show

Michaelmas Fair, Midsummer Common

Haddenham Steam Rally, Haddenham

Soham Pumpkin Fayre, Soham

October

Michaelmas Term begins

Duxford Airfield Air Show

World Conker Championship, Village Green, Ashton

November

Guy Fawkes Night: fair, stalls, a bonfire and fireworks, Midsummer Common

December

Varsity Rugby Match, Twickenham

Michaelmas Term ends

Pantomime

Festival of Nine Lessons and Carols, King's College Chapel

Guy Fawkes night

Rowing

Unless indicated otherwise, all telephone numbers in this guide should be prefixed by the area code 01223 when calling from outside Cambridge.

Emergency services

Ambulance, fire, police ☎ 999 (free service)

Addenbrooke's Hospital, Hills Road, Cambridge CB2 2QQ. Main switchboard ☎ 245151; Accident and Emergency Dept ☎ 217118

Dental Helpline. Weekdays only. ☎ 415126

Pharmacists. Out-of-hours opening times are on notices on pharmacies and in the local press.

Police Station, Parkside, Cambridge CB1 1JG ☎ 358966

Samaritans ☎ 364455

Access for people with a disability

Telephone numbers have been given throughout this guide for checking facilities in advance.

Please turn to the Getting Around section for further information under 'Disabled parking' and 'Shop-mobility'

Other useful numbers

Anglia Polytechnic University, East Road, Cambridge ☎ 363271

Automobile Association (AA), 24-hour breakdown service ☎ 0800 887766 (free)

BBC Radio Cambridgeshire, Broadcasting House, 104 Hills Road, Cambridge ☎ 259696/ 252000

Cambridgeshire Chamber of Commerce and Industry, The Business Centre, Station Road, Histon, Cambridge CB4 4LF ☎ 237414

Cambridge City Council, The Guildhall, Cambridge CB2 3QJ ☎ 457000

Cambridge Evening News, Winship Road, Milton ☎ 434434

Cambridge Health Authority ☎ 240782

Cambridgeshire County Council, Shire Hall, Castle Hill, Cambridge ☎ 717111

Central Library: Information Service and Cambridgeshire Collection, Lion Yard, Cambridge ☎ 712000

Citizens Advice Bureau ☎ 353875

Q 103 Radio, P.O. Box 1000, The Vision Park, Histon, Cambridge ☎ 235255/236103

Criminal courts: Crown Court ☎ 64436; Magistrates' Court ☎ 314311

East of England Tourist Board ☎ (01473) 822922

Open University (East Anglian Region), Cintra House, 12 Hills Road ☎ 364721

Post Office, General, 9–11 St Andrew's Street ☎ 323325

Record Office, The Shire Hall ☎ 717111

Royal Automobile Club (RAC), 24-hour breakdown service ☎ (0800) 828282 (free)

Tourist Information Centre, Wheeler Street, Cambridge CB2 3QB. Information: ☎ 322640; Fax 457588; Guided tours: ☎ 457574; Fax 457588; Conferences: ☎ 457577; Fax 457589

Town Crier, The Techno Park, Newmarket Road, Cambridge ☎ 369966

University of Cambridge:

University Offices, Old Schools, Trinity Lane, CB2 1TN ☎ 332200; enquiries 337733

American Friends of Cambridge University, Pitt Building, Trumpington Street ☎ 333315

Cambridge University Students' Union, 11–12 Trumpington Street ☎ 356454

Cambridge Union Society, 9A Bridge Street ☎ 566421

Intercollegiate Applications Office, Kellet Lodge, Tennis Court Road ☎ 333308

University Centre, Granta Place, Mill Lane ☎ 337766

Weather ☎ 0845 300300; recorded regional 5-day forecast 09003 406105

☐

Advertisers' index

Index

Pictures in *italic* type